BUT GOD

"The Battle Is Spiritual—But God Won the End From the Beginning."

PETER LENGWE

All Scripture quotations are taken from the New King James Version® (NKJV).

Printed in the United States of America

ISBN:
Softcover: 978-1-972299-78-4
Hardback: 978-1-972299-79-1
eBook: 978-1-972299-77-7

For permission requests, visit and write to the publisher at:

Peter Lengwe | THE BREAD OF LIFE GLOBAL MINISTRIES

ACKNOWLEDGMENTS

First and foremost,

To the Almighty God, my Father, my Shield, and my Deliverer:

All glory, honor, and praise belong to You alone.

You are the One who preserved me, sustained me, protected me, and empowered me to author this book.

Without Your grace, I would not be here.

Without Your Spirit, these pages would be empty.

Without Your mercy, this testimony would not exist.

You are the God who fought for me in battles seen and unseen.

You are the God who intervened when the enemy came in like a flood.

You are the God who spoke, guided, healed, restored, strengthened, and lifted me again and again.

This book is not my achievement—

it is Your victory in my life.

To Jesus Christ, my Savior, my Redeemer, my Lord:

Thank You for shedding Your blood,

for crushing the serpent's head,

for triumphing over darkness,

and for giving me life, hope, purpose, and destiny.

You are the center of every chapter, the anchor of every truth, and the reason I stand today.

Your love has been my strength.

Your presence has been my comfort.

Your victory is the assurance of my future.

To the Holy Spirit, my Helper, and my Teacher:

Thank You for revelation, insight, clarity, wisdom, and divine strength.

Thank You for stirring my heart to write,

for quickening the Word within me,

for empowering me in seasons of warfare,

and for making every chapter alive with spiritual truth.

This book breathes because You breathe through it.

To the warriors of faith who walked with me in spirit:

To the men and women of the Bible whose lives declare the triumph of God—

Abraham, Moses, David, Daniel, Esther, Job, Paul, and all who stood in the fire and did not bow.

Your stories have strengthened me through my darkest battles,

and your testimonies echo in these pages.

To the pastors, teachers, and servants of God who preach truth without compromise:

Thank you for your obedience in teaching the Gospel of Jesus Christ.

Your dedication to the Word has sharpened my understanding

and stirred my spirit to pursue deeper revelation.

Every seed of truth you planted has produced fruit in my life and in this work.

To every reader:

Thank you for opening your heart to the message God placed within these pages.

Thank you for your hunger to understand spiritual warfare,

for your courage to face your battles with faith,

and for your desire to walk in the victory Christ has already won for you.

May this book strengthen, empower, and awaken you

to the reality of the God who is fighting for you.

To those who prayed for me, encouraged me, and stood by me:

Your support has carried me in more ways than words can express.

Every prayer, every word of encouragement, every gesture of kindness

has been a reminder that God surrounds His chosen with people of faith.

Thank you for believing in the calling God has placed on my life.

To the adversities I faced along the way:

Though painful, they drove me deeper into God.

Every attack trained my hands for war.

Every storm taught me to trust.

Every tear watered the soil of this calling.

To the enemy of my soul:

You tried—

but God.

You attacked—

but God.

You plotted—

but God.

You pushed—

but God.

You lost—

because God wins every time.

Finally,

To everyone who will read this book long after it is written:

May you know this truth with absolute certainty:

The battle is spiritual,

but God won the end from the beginning.

To Him be all the glory,

forever and ever.

Amen.

PREFACE

There are moments in life when the battle becomes so fierce, so unrelenting, that you can almost feel the breath of darkness against your soul. Moments when the attacks seem coordinated, intentional, and targeted—not random, not accidental, not mere coincidence. Moments when the enemy's goal is clear: to silence you, break you, and derail the purpose of God in your life.

I have lived through such moments.

There were seasons when the enemy rose violently against my calling, my peace, and even my sanity. Times when I felt surrounded on every side, facing battles I could not explain, attacks I did not provoke, and storms I did not invite. Yet in all those moments, one truth kept rising above every voice of fear, every threat of darkness, and every weapon formed against me:

"Unless the LORD had been my help, my soul would soon have settled in silence."

— Psalm 94:17 (NKJV)

If the Lord had not intervened…

If His grace had not held me…

If His hand had not fought for me…

I would not be writing these words today.

This book was born out of warfare, but also out of victory. Out of battles I could not win on my own, but also out of testimonies that only the hand of God could produce. It was in those dark hours that one truth became unshakably clear to me:

The battle is spiritual—but God won the end from the beginning.

From Genesis to Revelation, this divine pattern repeats over and over. Every time Satan rises to stop God's purpose, God rises higher. Every time darkness launches an attack, light breaks through. Every time the enemy targets God's chosen ones, heaven responds with power, authority, and intervention.

BUT GOD — these two words echo through Scripture like a thunderstorm of hope.

- Joseph was betrayed… but God elevated him.
- Israel was trapped at the Red Sea… but God opened it.
- David stood before Goliath… but God strengthened him.
- Daniel was thrown to lions… but God shut their mouths.
- The disciples feared for their lives… but God calmed the storm.
- Jesus was crucified… but God raised Him on the third day.

The same God who intervened then…

intervenes now.

This book is a journey through the battles of God's chosen ones—men, women, and entire nations whom the devil tried to stop, destroy, silence, or erase. You will see the war behind their war, the invisible conflict behind their visible trials, and the supernatural intervention that turned the outcome in their favor.

But more importantly, this book will reveal the One who stands at the center of every victory—Jesus Christ, the Light of the world, the Captain of our salvation, and the One who conquered the powers of darkness once and for all.

My prayer is that as you read, scales will fall from your eyes. That you will begin to see your battles the way heaven sees them. That you will understand that nothing that rises against you begins on earth—every battle begins in the spirit, and every victory is secured in the spirit before it ever manifests in the natural.

May this book remind you that you are not abandoned, not unprotected, not defenseless.

You are chosen.

You are covered.

You are fought for.

You are upheld by the God who wrote your ending before your beginning.

And no matter what rises against you—

BUT GOD will rise higher.

INTRODUCTION

"The Battle Is Spiritual—But God Won the End From the Beginning."

Every believer who has ever walked with God has faced a moment when the attacks felt too calculated to be ordinary, too strategic to be natural, and too heavy to be human. That is because the greatest battles of your life are not fought on earth first—they are fought in the spirit.

Behind every sickness, every sudden storm, every betrayal, every delay, every trap, and every assignment of destruction, there is a real enemy with a real agenda. His purpose is singular: to oppose the will of God, attack the chosen of God, and frustrate the purpose of God.

But while the enemy fights you because of your future, God defends you because of His plan.

This book begins by unveiling that truth. The battles you face are not just about you—they are about what God wants to accomplish through you. They are about the glory God will reveal, the destiny He has written, and the impact your life will have in the kingdom of God.

The Invisible War Behind Every Visible Attack

The Bible is clear:

"We do not wrestle against flesh and blood..." (Ephesians 6:12, NKJV).

You are not fighting people.

You are not fighting circumstances.

You are not fighting situations.

You are encountering the conflict between two kingdoms:

- The kingdom of darkness, where Satan and his forces operate.
- The kingdom of light, where God reigns and angels are dispatched.

What manifests on earth is simply the fruit of what has already taken place in the spirit. This is why your battles feel spiritual—because they are.

This explains why:

- Pharaoh tried to kill Moses before he grew.
- Saul hunted David before he sat on the throne.
- Haman plotted genocide against Israel before deliverance came.
- Herod killed infants to stop Jesus before His ministry began.

Satan always attacks at the brink of manifestation—because he fears what God is about to release.

Why God's Chosen Ones Are Always Targeted

When God chooses a man or woman, hell takes notice.

Your calling attracts conflict.

Your purpose attracts pressure.

Your anointing attracts opposition.

You are targeted not because you are weak—but because you are marked.

Just as God uses people to fulfill His will, Satan uses people to fight that will.

Just as angels work on God's behalf, demons resist what God is doing.

This book exposes that spiritual reality while reminding you of a greater truth:

No weapon formed can prosper against what God has ordained.

The Central Theme: BUT GOD

Throughout Scripture, every time the enemy lifted his hand to destroy God's chosen ones, heaven lifted a hand to intervene. The Bible is not the story of human struggle—it is the story of divine rescue. It is the story of a God who steps into the fiercest battles of His children and overturns the enemy's plans.

It is the story of BUT GOD moments.

- The enemy planned death for Joseph—but God planned destiny.
- The furnace threatened to consume the three Hebrew boys—but God walked with them.
- Daniel's enemies conspired—but God sent His angel.
- Satan entered Judas—but God still accomplished redemption.

And above all:

- Darkness crucified Jesus—but God raised Him from the dead.

The victory of Christ is the ultimate "BUT GOD."

It is the proof that God always writes the final chapter.

What This Book Will Reveal

This book will take you through the Scriptures to show:

- Why the devil fights the purpose of God
- How spiritual attacks originate
- How angels fight on behalf of God's people
- Why nothing happens physically until it happens spiritually
- How God intervenes in impossible situations
- How His chosen ones always come out victorious
- Why your story is already written from beginning to end
- And why no attack can stop what God has ordained

More importantly, it will point you to Jesus Christ, who crushed the serpent, defeated death, disarmed principalities, and secured eternal victory for all who belong to Him.

Your Life Will Never Look the Same After This

As you read, you will begin to see your battles differently.

You will realize you are not alone.

You will understand why you were attacked.

You will see how heaven fights for you.

And you will discover that every attack is simply the enemy's fear of what God has already destined for your life.

By the end of this journey, you will stand with confidence and declare:

"The battle is spiritual—but God won the end from the beginning."

And you will know in your spirit:

If God is for me, then nothing—seen or unseen—can stop His purpose in my life.

ABOUT THE AUTHOR

Peter Lengwe is a devoted servant of the Lord Jesus Christ, a passionate student of the Word, and a man whose life testifies to the power, mercy, and faithfulness of God. Marked by deep spiritual insight and a profound understanding of Scripture, Peter writes with clarity, conviction, and an unwavering commitment to truth.

His journey has not been easy.

From childhood to adulthood, Peter has walked through intense spiritual battles, seasons of crushing pressure, unexpected storms, and moments of overwhelming darkness. Yet through it all, one truth has carried him:

BUT GOD.

God preserved him when the enemy sought to destroy him.

God guided him when paths were uncertain.

God strengthened him when he was weak.

God covered him when he was surrounded.

God lifted him when he fell.

God restored him when others counted him out.

And God raised him for such a time as this.

Today, Peter writes not from theory, but from experience—

from fire-tested faith,

from warfare survived,

and from revelation birthed in prayer and tears.

His books are written to teach, encourage, and awaken believers to the reality of spiritual warfare and the victory Christ has already secured for His people. Whether explaining prophecy, unveiling biblical mysteries, or guiding readers through the battles of life, Peter's passion is always the same:

To exalt Jesus Christ,

to strengthen the Church,

and to reveal the God who wins every battle from the beginning to the end.

Peter believes that Scripture must be understood deeply, applied faithfully, and lived courageously. His writing reflects a unique blend of:

- biblical teaching,
- prophetic insight,
- real-life experience,
- spiritual revelation,
- and the empowering presence of the Holy Spirit.

Every message he shares carries the heartbeat of one who has walked through the fire but emerged with a testimony of God's enduring love and power.

When Peter is not writing, he is studying the Word, praying, and encouraging others to grow in their faith. His desire is that every believer would know the God who defended David, delivered Daniel, preserved Esther, restored Job, and raised Jesus from the dead—

because that same God fights for us today.

Peter's life, ministry, and books are a living declaration that:

The battle is spiritual—

but God won the end from the beginning.

TABLE OF CONTENTS

CHAPTER ONE: THE FIRST REBELLION: WHEN SATAN ROSE AGAINST THE WILL OF GOD

Before the Garden…

Before Adam…

Before the creation of man…

There was another beginning.

A beginning marked not by light, but by rebellion.

Not by obedience, but by pride.

Not by worship, but by war.

This was the first battle ever fought—

a heavenly revolt against the will and purpose of God.

Everything we see on earth today—temptation, deception, spiritual warfare, demonic opposition—began not on earth, but in heaven itself.

1. Lucifer: Created to Reveal the Glory of God

Before he was Satan, the adversary…

Before he was the serpent who deceived Eve…

He was Lucifer, the anointed cherub.

Scripture reveals that he was:

- Created in beauty (Ezekiel 28:12)
- Covered in precious stones (Ezekiel 28:13)
- Perfect in his ways from the day he was created (Ezekiel 28:15)
- A guardian cherub who stood in the presence of God (Ezekiel 28:14)

Lucifer's original purpose was holy:

to reflect the glory of God.

He was created to magnify God, not himself.

But pride corrupted what God created pure.

2. Pride: The Seed of Rebellion

Lucifer's downfall began with a desire that did not come from heaven—

a desire to replace God instead of reflecting Him.

In Isaiah 14:13–14, we see the five statements of Satan's rebellion:

- “I will ascend into heaven.”
- “I will exalt my throne above the stars of God.”
- “I will sit on the mount of the congregation.”
- “I will ascend above the heights of the clouds.”
- “I will be like the Most High.”

Every “I will” challenged God’s will.

Every desire was a direct attack on God’s purpose.

His rebellion was not simply pride—it was war against the very plan of God.

Lucifer wanted the throne.

He wanted worship.

He wanted authority.

He wanted the glory that belonged to God alone.

This was the first spiritual coup attempt.

The first cosmic rebellion.

The first direct challenge to the sovereignty of God.

3. Why Satan Rebelled Against the Will and Purpose of God

God has always had a purpose—

a plan to fill heaven and earth with His glory through His creation.

He created angels as heavenly servants.

He created man as His earthly image-bearers.

He created order, harmony, unity, and worship.

Lucifer's rebellion aimed to destroy all of this.

His rebellion was an attempt to:

- Overthrow the government of Heaven
- Interrupt the worship of angels
- Redirect glory to himself
- Challenge the authority of God
- Derail God's eternal purpose

Satan's goal has always been the same:

To stop the will of God from manifesting in heaven and on earth.

What he failed to accomplish in heaven, he tried to accomplish on earth.

4. The War in Heaven: When Darkness Rose Against Light

Revelation 12 :7–9 reveals the cosmic war:

"And war broke out in heaven: Michael and his angels fought with the dragon;

and the dragon and his angels fought..."

One-third of the angels joined Lucifer's rebellion.

Heaven was shaken, but heaven did not fall.

Because…

Light always triumphs over darkness.

Truth always overcomes deception.

God's will always prevail.

Michael, the warrior archangel, rose with the forces of God.

The Bible says:

"...but they did not prevail..." (Revelation 12 :8)

Hell has never prevailed over heaven.

Darkness has never won against God.

Evil has never overpowered righteousness.

Lucifer was cast out.

Fallen.

Defeated.

Disarmed.

Expelled from the presence of God.

But he was not done fighting.

5. Satan's Strategy After His Fall: Stop God's Purpose on Earth

When Satan failed to overthrow God in heaven,

he turned his rage toward the next expression of God's purpose:

humanity.

Why?

Because man was made in God's image.

Because man was given authority on earth.

Because man was chosen to walk in fellowship with God.

Because man would carry the lineage through which Christ would come.

So, the rebellion that began in heaven…

continued in the garden.

The war against God's will moved from the heavenly realm…

to the earthly realm.

Just as Satan sought to dethrone God in heaven…

he sought to dethrone God's purpose in Adam.

That's why he targeted Eve.

That's why he deceived humanity.

That's why he sought to corrupt what God created good.

Satan's fall became humanity's first spiritual threat.

And the battle that began with angels…

…continued with Adam and Eve.

6. Heaven's Response: God's Purpose Cannot Be Destroyed

Satan's rebellion did not change God's plan.

It only revealed God's power.

The enemy's fall did not disturb God's throne.

It only displayed His sovereignty.

Even after Lucifer rebelled…

Even after he deceived Eve…

Even after Adam fell…

God still declared:

"My purpose shall stand." (Isaiah 46:10)

The enemy tried to stop God's purpose in heaven—

but God cast him out.

He tried to stop God's purpose in the garden—

but God promised the Seed.

He tried to stop God's purpose in Israel—

but God preserved a remnant.

He tried to stop God's purpose through Christ—

but God raised Him from the dead.

And today, the enemy may try to stop God's purpose in your life…

but God has already written your ending from your beginning.

7. The Message of the First War

The fall of Satan and the fall of Adam stand as twin testimonies of one eternal truth:

The battle is spiritual —

but God's purpose always prevails.

Satan can rebel, but God remains enthroned.

Satan can deceive, but God will intervene.

Satan can attack, but God will protect.

Satan can strategize, but God will overturn.

And the war that began in heaven continues on earth—

but the victory has always belonged to God.

CHAPTER TWO: ADAM AND EVE: THE BEGINNING OF THE BATTLE ON THE EARTH BETWEEN LIGHT AND DARKNESS

When Adam and Eve fell, God did not abandon His purpose.

He did not change His plan.

He did not surrender humanity to darkness.

Instead, God revealed the first prophecy of hope — the promise of the Seed who would crush the serpent's head (Genesis 3:15).

That promise made Satan furious.

Because Satan understood this:

If the Seed is born, his kingdom is finished.

If the Seed comes, his head will be crushed.

If the Seed arrives, the purpose of God will triumph forever.

And so, Satan turned his focus to the next battlefield:

the children of Adam.

1. Cain and Abel: Two Sons, Two Paths, Two Destinies

Adam and Eve had two sons:

- Cain, a tiller of the ground
- Abel, a keeper of the sheep

Both brought offerings to God —

but only one offering was accepted.

Why?

Because Abel approached God in faith and obedience (Hebrews 11:4),

while Cain approached God on his own terms.

Abel honored the will of God.

Cain rejected it.

And immediately we see the same war that began in heaven

and continued in Eden

now rise again between two brothers.

One reflected the light.

One embraced darkness.

One walked in obedience.

One walked in rebellion.

One aligned with God's purpose.

One opened himself to the enemy's influence.

This was not simply a family disagreement.

It was spiritual warfare.

2. Why Satan Targeted Abel

If God accepted Abel's worship…

If God favored Abel's faith…

If Abel walked in righteousness…

then Abel's lineage was a threat to Satan's plan.

Because the Seed — the Messiah — would eventually come through a righteous line.

Abel represented God's chosen path.

Cain represented human will over God's will.

Satan saw what God saw —

that Abel's heart aligned with heaven.

And so, the enemy whispered envy, jealousy, and anger into Cain.

The Bible says:

"And Cain was very angry, and his countenance fell."

(Genesis 4:5)

The same spirit that moved Satan in heaven

now moved Cain on earth.

The same desire to oppose God's will

now rose through Cain against Abel.

Satan could not stop God's purpose in heaven,

so, he tried to stop it through human vessels on earth.

3. Sin at the Door: The First Spiritual Warning

Before Cain acted, God warned him:

"Sin lies at the door.

And its desire is for you,

but you should rule over it."

(Genesis 4:7)

Notice:

- God did not say "sin is inside you"
- He said "sin is at the door" — a spiritual presence
- "Its desire is for you" — a demonic intention
- "You should rule over it" — spiritual authority

This is the first direct biblical description of spiritual warfare affecting human behavior.

God revealed that the battle around Cain was not merely emotional —

it was demonic influence seeking entry.

Cain's anger was the doorway.

Envy was the foothold.

Offense was the crack Satan needed.

The same pattern exists today:

Satan waits at the doors of anger, bitterness, and offense,

hoping to enter and use people to oppose the will of God.

4. The First Murder: The First Attempt to Crush God's Purpose

Cain attacked Abel in the field and killed him (Genesis 4:8).

But this was not mere murder.

It was the first attempt to stop the prophetic Seed.

Abel was the righteous lineage —

and Satan sought to cut it off.

In that moment, darkness celebrated again.

Hell rejoiced.

The enemy believed he had destroyed the chosen path for God's purpose.

But as always…

BUT GOD.

5. BUT GOD Raised Another Seed

God had already written the ending from the beginning.

Abel died,

but the purpose of God did not.

The Seed was bruised,

but the promise stood firm.

And God intervened:

"And Adam knew his wife again, and she bore a son and named him Seth,

'For God has appointed another seed for me instead of Abel, whom Cain killed.'"

(Genesis 4:25)

Look at that:

"...another seed..."

God always preserves His purpose.

Hell killed Abel,

but God raised Seth.

The serpent struck,

but God positioned a new lineage.

Satan's plan failed before it began.

Because no attack—seen or unseen—can overturn what God has ordained.

6. Seth: The Continuation of God's Plan

Through Seth, God continued the righteous line.

The lineage flowed from Seth...

to Enosh...

to Enoch...

to Noah…

and eventually all the way to:

- Abraham
- Isaac
- Jacob
- Judah
- David
- and Jesus Christ, the promised Seed

What Satan tried to stop with Abel,

God continued through Seth.

The plan of God cannot be killed.

The purpose of God cannot be interrupted.

The promise of God cannot be silenced.

Because the battle is spiritual—

but God won the end from the beginning.

7. The Message of Cain and Abel for Us Today

From the very beginning, Scripture shows:

- Satan uses people to fight God's purpose
- God raises new vessels when the enemy attacks
- Darkness strikes, but light always rises
- The enemy can delay but cannot destroy

- God’s purpose continues through vessels of obedience
- And God’s plan always moves forward

Your calling is not fragile.

Your purpose is not breakable.

Your destiny is not vulnerable.

What God ordains,

no scheme of hell can overturn.

The battle began in heaven…

continued in Eden…

manifested in Cain and Abel…

And continues in every generation—

including ours.

CHAPTER THREE: THE RISE OF CORRUPTION BEFORE THE FLOOD

"But Noah found grace in the eyes of the LORD." — Genesis 6:8 (NKJV)

The story of Cain and Abel showed Satan's first attempt to interfere with God's purpose through the children of Adam.

But the enemy did not stop there.

What began as a single act of violence escalated into a global strategy.

The battlefield widened.

The war intensified.

Darkness began to spread like a disease across humanity.

And once again, the purpose of God was at stake.

1. From One Murder to a Civilization of Violence

The murder of Abel was only the beginning.

Cain, now hardened by rebellion, went out from the presence of the Lord (Genesis 4:16) and built a city.

A civilization rooted not in the fear of God,

but in human pride,

human strength,

and human ambition.

Cain's descendants show a rapid decay:

- Lamech, the first man to take two wives
- Lamech, the first man to boast in murder
- A culture of vengeance, pride, and violence
- A people inventing weapons and worldly pleasures
- A society moving farther and farther from God

Everything God desired—righteousness, fellowship, holiness—

was replaced with corruption, arrogance, and bloodshed.

The enemy expanded his influence.

But this was only the beginning of his strategy.

2. A Deeper Invasion: The Sons of God and the Daughters of Men

Genesis 6 reveals one of the most mysterious and severe moments in Scripture:

"The sons of God saw the daughters of men, that they were beautiful; and they took wives for themselves..."

(Genesis 6:2)

These "sons of God" were fallen angels —

rebellious spiritual beings who left their proper domain (Jude 6).

Their purpose?

To corrupt the human bloodline

and contaminate the lineage through which the Seed — the Messiah — would come.

This was not random wickedness.

It was a targeted satanic attack.

The plan was simple:

If Satan could contaminate humanity,

he could prevent the birth of the pure, promised Seed

that would crush his head.

This was an attempt at total spiritual sabotage.

3. The Result: A Corrupted, Violent, Demonically Influenced World

The union between fallen angels and human women produced giants — the Nephilim (Genesis 6:4).

These beings were fierce, violent, and oppressive.

The world became:

- Filled with bloodshed
- Filled with demonic influence
- Filled with sexual perversion
- Filled with rebellion against God
- Filled with corrupted flesh
- Filled with spiritual darkness

Genesis 6:5 describes humanity in the darkest terms:

"Every intent of the thoughts of his heart was only evil continually."

Imagine that:

every thought

every imagination

every desire

pointed to darkness.

The enemy had almost achieved his plan.

Humanity—created in God's image—was on the brink of total spiritual collapse.

The purpose of God appeared threatened.

But God had a plan the enemy did not expect.

4. BUT GOD: A Remnant of Righteousness in the Midst of Corruption

Just when it looked like darkness had consumed the earth…

just when the enemy's strategy seemed unstoppable…

just when the purpose of God seemed lost…

"But Noah found grace in the eyes of the LORD."

(Genesis 6:8)

Those two words — "But Noah" — change everything.

Noah was:

- Righteous
- Blameless in his generation
- A man who walked with God
  (Genesis 6:9)

Despite the rampant corruption,

God preserved one man, one family, one lineage

through which His purpose would continue.

The Seed was safe.

The plan of redemption remained intact.

Satan had corrupted the world,

but God preserved a remnant.

5. The Ark: God's Answer to Satan's Attack

God instructed Noah to build an ark:

- A vessel of salvation
- A symbol of divine preservation
- A testimony that God's purpose cannot be destroyed

- A warning to the world
- A shelter for the chosen

When the flood came,

it was not just judgment —

it was protection.

God removed the corruption,

preserved the righteous,

and reset the stage for His plan to continue.

Every swing of Noah's hammer

was a declaration to the powers of darkness:

"You will not stop the purpose of God."

6. The Flood: A Spiritual Reset

When the waters rose,

the world of violence, corruption, and demonic influence was washed away.

Satan's strategy failed.

His attempt to corrupt the human lineage failed.

His plan to prevent the coming of Christ failed.

Noah stepped out of the ark onto new ground.

A new beginning.

A preserved lineage.

The continuation of God's purpose.

Once again, the message was clear:

The battle is spiritual —

but God won the end from the beginning.

7. The Lesson for Us Today

The days before the flood reveal timeless truths:

- Satan seeks to corrupt what God has chosen.
- Darkness always tries to fill the earth.
- Demonic influence increases when people forget God.
- Corruption spreads when spiritual vigilance is lost.
- But God always preserves a remnant.
- God always has a Noah.
- God always keeps His purpose alive.
- And God always intervenes before His plan is destroyed.

The flood was not God giving up —

it was God ensuring His purpose would stand forever.

CHAPTER FOUR: ABRAHAM: WHEN DESTINY IS CONTESTED

"Is anything too hard for the LORD?" — Genesis 18:14 (NKJV)

When God chose Abraham, the war intensified.

Because choosing Abraham meant choosing a nation,

a covenant,

a lineage,

and a future through which the Messiah would come.

The enemy understood this clearly:

If Abraham fulfills his purpose, the plan of redemption will unfold.

So, from the moment God called Abraham, Satan moved to resist him.

This was not just the story of a man —

it was the story of a destiny Satan could not afford to let succeed.

1. The Call of God — And the Immediate War Against It

When God called Abram out of Ur, He spoke destiny:

- "I will make you a great nation."
- "I will bless you."
- "I will make your name great."
- "In you all the families of the earth shall be blessed." (Genesis 12:2–3)

This blessing pointed to something much bigger than land or descendants…

It pointed to Christ,

the "Seed" who would come through Abraham (Galatians 3:16).

And the enemy knew:

Abraham is the chosen vessel for God's redemptive plan.

So, the attacks began.

You will always know your calling is real

by the size of the warfare that rises against it.

2. The Strategy of Delay — Barrenness in Sarah

The first major attack on Abraham's destiny was barrenness.

Sarah could not conceive.

The womb that was chosen to carry the promise was shut.

This was not natural —

it was a spiritual resistance.

Barrenness is often Satan's strategy to:

- Delay God's timing
- Create frustration
- Produce unbelief
- Push people toward human solutions
- Break unity in marriage
- Misalign God's perfect will

Satan wasn't after Sarah's womb…

he was after God's promise.

If Sarah could not give birth,

then the Seed could not continue.

No Isaac.

No Jacob.

No Judah.

No David.

No Jesus.

That was the enemy's target.

3. The Attack of Fear — Famine in the Land

Immediately after Abraham obeyed God, famine struck the land (Genesis 12:10).

Famine tests:

- Faith
- Trust
- Obedience
- Dependence on God

And it raises questions:

"Did God really call me?"

"Did I make a mistake?"

"Should I turn back?"

But every famine in Scripture is a spiritual attack on destiny.

Satan wants to push God's chosen ones out of position

so, they miss the place where the blessing will manifest.

Abraham went to Egypt,

and that decision led to another attack.

4. The Attack of Fear & Compromise — Sarah in Pharaoh's House

In Egypt, Abraham feared for his life.

Fear opens the door to compromise.

Compromise opens the door to spiritual vulnerability.

Pharaoh took Sarah into his house —

the woman chosen to carry the promise.

This was not accidental.

It was spiritual warfare.

If Sarah became defiled,

the purity of the lineage through which the Messiah would come

would be corrupted.

The enemy tried to contaminate the covenant before Isaac could be born.

But then…

BUT GOD.

God intervened supernaturally:

- He struck Pharaoh's household with plagues
- He exposed the situation
- He restored Sarah untouched
- He protected the covenant lineage

The plans of darkness failed.

5. The Counterfeit Strategy — Hagar and Ishmael

Delay can pressure even the righteous into creating counterfeit solutions.

After years of barrenness,

Sarah and Abraham agreed to conceive through Hagar.

Ishmael was born—

not a mistake,

but not the promise.

Satan knew something:

If he could produce a counterfeit son,

he could confuse the covenant.

And Ishmael became:

- A source of conflict
- A source of division
- A parallel lineage
- A distraction from God's original plan

But God made it clear:

"In Isaac your seed shall be called."

(Genesis 21:12)

Satan brought confusion,

but God clarified the covenant.

The promise remained on Isaac.

6. The Renewed Attack — Laughter and Unbelief

When God said Sarah would conceive, she laughed —

not out of joy, but disbelief.

This was spiritual warfare in the mind.

The enemy attacks faith because faith receives the promise.

But God confronted the unbelief:

"Is anything too hard for the LORD?"

(Genesis 18:14)

That question destroys every attack of doubt.

And at the appointed time,

Sarah conceived.

Destiny was birthed.

7. The Promise Arrives — Isaac Is Born

Isaac — the son of laughter.

Isaac — the child of promise.

Isaac — the continuation of the Seed.

Isaac — the proof that God's Word never fails.

Everything Satan tried to stop

God fulfilled.

Because when the purpose of God is at stake:

- Delay cannot stop it
- Barrenness cannot stop it
- Fear cannot stop it
- Pharaoh cannot stop it
- Counterfeits cannot stop it
- Unbelief cannot stop it
- Time cannot stop it

BUT GOD always brings His Word to pass.

8. The Test — Abraham and Isaac on Mount Moriah

One more attack rose —

not from Satan directly,

but as a test of Abraham's loyalty.

God asked Abraham to sacrifice Isaac.

This was the spiritual climax of Abraham's journey.

If Isaac died,

the covenant died.

The lineage died.

The Seed died.

But Abraham's faith was stronger than death.

He believed that if Isaac died,

God would raise him up

(Hebrews 11:17–19).

And at the very moment the knife was raised…

BUT GOD intervened.

A ram was provided.

The covenant was preserved.

The promise continued.

And God revealed Himself as Jehovah Jireh — The Lord Who Provides.

9. The Message of Abraham's Story

Abraham's journey teaches us:

- The greater your calling, the greater the warfare
- Every divine purpose will be contested
- Delay is not denial — it is spiritual resistance
- God protects whatever He promises
- Counterfeits cannot cancel the true plan of God
- Every attack becomes a testimony
- Faith is the key to sustaining destiny
- God always steps in on time

And ultimately:

The battle is spiritual —

but God won the end from the beginning.

CHAPTER FIVE: JOSEPH: WHEN EVIL TRIES TO REWRITE YOUR STORY BUT GOD TURNS IT FOR GOOD

"But as for you, you meant evil against me; but God meant it for good." — Genesis 50:20 (NKJV)

Joseph's story is not simply the journey of a young man from the pit to the palace —

it is the revelation of how spiritual warfare follows every God-given destiny,

and how God intervenes at every level of the attack.

Joseph's life shows us this truth:

The deeper the calling, the fiercer the warfare.

The greater the destiny, the stronger the attack.

Because Joseph was chosen to preserve the nation of Israel

— and the lineage of the Messiah —

Satan targeted him with relentless precision.

1. The Dream: When Destiny Is Revealed, War Begins

Joseph was seventeen when God revealed his future through dreams.

The dreams showed:

- Elevation
- Authority
- Influence
- Leadership
- Destiny

But destiny always attracts opposition.

Once Joseph saw his future,

Satan saw it too.

The enemy understood what many believers don't realize:

The moment God speaks, Satan strikes.

Why?

Because dreams are spiritual blueprints of destiny.

And when God reveals the plan,

the enemy begins to fight that plan.

2. Jealousy in the House: The Enemy Uses Those Closest to You

Joseph's own brothers hated him:

- because he was favored
- because he was gifted
- because he was anointed
- because of the dreams God gave him

This shows an important principle:

Satan often starts his attacks in the environment closest to your calling.

The first opposition Joseph faced wasn't from Egypt…

it was from his own family.

Enemies outside cannot stop you

until envy inside revolts against you.

Why?

Because familiar voices can wound deeper than foreign ones.

Joseph's brothers became instruments in the enemy's hand.

But they did not know

that every act of hatred would only push Joseph closer to his destiny.

3. The Plot to Kill Joseph — An Attempt to Abort the Purpose

The brothers said:

"Come therefore, let us now kill him…"

(Genesis 37:20)

This was more than sibling rivalry —

it was Satan attempting to kill the destiny God placed on Joseph.

Joseph's life represented:

- the future preservation of Israel
- the continuation of the promised lineage
- the protection of the covenant people
- the plan that would lead to Christ

So Satan's goal was clear:

Kill the dream.

Kill the dreamer.

Kill the purpose.

But there was one problem:

Joseph's purpose was already written by God.

And Satan cannot kill what God has already ordained to live.

4. The Pit: When the Enemy Thinks It Has Won

Joseph was stripped of his coat —

the symbol of favor.

Thrown into a pit —

the symbol of rejection.

The enemy celebrated.

It looked like:

- The dream was dead
- The promise was gone
- The purpose was crushed
- Joseph's destiny was buried

But the pit was not the end —

it was the first step toward the throne.

What the enemy meant as a grave,

God meant as a gateway.

Every destiny must pass through a pit

so that pride is broken

and dependence on God is born.

5. Sold Into Slavery — An Attack on Identity

Joseph was sold for twenty pieces of silver.

To the enemy, this was victory.

To God, this was positioning.

Slavery was designed to:

- break Joseph's identity
- strip him of worth
- crush his confidence
- push him into despair

But through it,

Joseph was being moved into the exact place

where his destiny would unfold.

Sometimes God lets the enemy move you

so that you arrive exactly where He wants you.

Even when people sell you out,

they are transporting you to your purpose.

6. Potiphar's House — When Temptation Targets Your Purpose

In Egypt, Joseph rose in Potiphar's house.

But as soon as he prospered,

another attack came.

Potiphar's wife targeted Joseph

— not because he was handsome alone —

but because he was destined.

Satan uses temptation

to contaminate vessels chosen by God.

If Joseph fell here:

- his integrity would be destroyed
- his reputation ruined
- his credibility broken
- his destiny delayed

- his influence reduced

The enemy wanted to stain the vessel

that God wanted to elevate.

But Joseph said:

"How then can I do this great wickedness and sin against God?"

(Genesis 39:9)

This was not willpower —

it was spiritual warfare.

Joseph refused the temporary pleasure

to preserve the eternal purpose.

7. False Accusation — When Lies Become Weapons

Potiphar's wife lied.

Joseph was falsely accused.

He was thrown into prison.

Another attack.

Another spiritual blow.

The enemy used:

- lies
- Manipulation
- injustice
- false witnesses

- Slander

All designed to destroy Joseph's ascent.

But the enemy did not know

that prison was not a prison — it was a pathway.

The darkest rooms often hide the brightest doors.

8. Prison — When You Are Hidden but Not Forgotten

In prison, Joseph :

- interpreted dreams
- walked in integrity
- remained faithful
- grew in wisdom
- was refined by suffering

He was hidden,

but God was preparing him.

When God hides you,

it is never punishment —

it is preparation.

Joseph was not waiting for Pharaoh —

Pharaoh was waiting for Joseph.

9. The Moment of Elevation — God's Intervention in Due Season

Pharaoh dreamed.

No one could interpret it.

Except Joseph.

In one day —

from prisoner to prime minister.

From forgotten to favored.

From bound to elevated.

Because when God decides it's time,

no man, no prison, no lie, no chain, no demon

can stop the hand of God.

Joseph was placed in the exact position

to preserve the nation during famine.

Why?

Because through Israel would come Judah.

Through Judah — David.

Through David — Jesus.

God raised Joseph

to protect the lineage of Christ.

This was not politics —

it was prophecy.

10. Joseph's Revelation — Seeing the Hand of God Behind the Warfare

When Joseph's brothers bowed before him —

as God once showed him in dreams —

Joseph understood everything.

He said:

"You meant evil against me;

but God meant it for good,

in order to bring it about as it is this day,

to save many people alive."

(Genesis 50:20)

This is the anthem of the entire book:

The enemy meant evil —

but God had a purpose.

The pit meant destruction —

but God meant promotion.

The prison meant delay —

but God meant preparation.

The betrayal meant brokenness —

but God meant positioning.

Joseph's story reveals the eternal truth:

The battle is spiritual —

but God won the end from the beginning.

CHAPTER SIX: MOSES: THE DELIVERER HELL TRIED TO KILL

"For the LORD will fight for you, and you shall hold your peace." — Exodus 14:14 (NKJV)

Whenever God raises a deliverer…

Hell raises a destroyer.

Whenever God begins a new move…

Satan begins a new attack.

Moses' story is one of the clearest demonstrations of how the enemy tries to eliminate the vessel before the assignment begins — because the enemy knows what the vessel will become.

1. Israel in Egypt — A Growing Threat to the Kingdom of Darkness

Israel was not in Egypt by accident.

They were there because of Joseph's obedience and God's sovereign plan.

But as Israel multiplied:

- Darkness became threatened
- Egypt became fearful
- Pharaoh became oppressive

Israel represented more than a nation —

they represented the line through which Christ would come.

And Satan knew:

If Israel grows, the promise grows.

If Israel prospers, the covenant prospers.

So, the enemy stirred Pharaoh's heart to oppress God's people.

The slavery of Israel was not merely political —

it was spiritual warfare.

2. Pharaoh's Decree — Satan's Attempt at Genocide

Pharaoh commanded:

"Every son who is born you shall cast into the river..."

(Exodus 1:22)

This was not just cruelty —

it was a demonic attempt to cut off the deliverer God would raise.

Three things reveal the spiritual nature behind Pharaoh's decree:

1. It targeted males only

Because Moses was male.

2. It targeted newborns

Because the enemy always attacks purpose in its infancy.

3. It used water

Because water represented cleansing and judgment —

Satan attempted to turn God's symbol into a weapon of destruction.

This was history's first attempt to kill Moses

before he ever drew breath into destiny.

The same strategy Satan used later with Herod to try to kill Jesus.

3. BUT GOD — Moses Is Hidden Under Divine Protection

When the enemy plans destruction…

God plans deliverance.

When the enemy releases a decree…

God releases a way of escape.

Moses' mother hid him for three months.

That was not just bravery —

it was divine guidance.

When she placed him in a basket,

she was placing him:

- into destiny
- into protection
- into God's hands

The basket floated where God needed Moses to be.

Not one wave could overturn it.

Not one ripple could threaten it.

Not one crocodile could approach it.

Because the hand of God was under the basket.

4. Pharaoh's Daughter — The Miracle No Demon Could Stop

Here is the most astonishing part:

The very household that issued the decree to kill Hebrew boys

became the household that preserved the future deliverer.

This is the brilliance of God:

He hides His purpose in the enemy's house,

and the enemy cannot see it.

Pharaoh paid for Moses' clothes…

fed him…

educated him…

raised him…

trained him.

Hell planned to kill Moses

but God used hell's resources to prepare him.

This is why Scripture says:

"You prepare a table before me in the presence of my enemies."

(Psalm 23:5)

5. Moses Trained in Egypt — God Preparing His Vessel

While in Pharaoh's house, Moses learned:

- leadership
- discipline
- strategy
- warfare
- Administration
- royal protocol
- Egyptian wisdom

Everything he learned in Egypt

would be needed to confront Egypt.

God trains His warriors in the territory of their future assignment.

6. Moses' Failure and Running to Midian — A Spiritual Attack of Condemnation

Moses killed an Egyptian and fled into the wilderness.

This was another attack:

- Shame

- Condemnation
- Confusion
- Identity crisis
- Fear
- Delay

But even here:

Moses was not running from destiny —

he was running into preparation.

The wilderness was not a punishment…

it was a classroom.

The prince had to die

so, the shepherd could rise.

God was stripping Moses of Egypt

to clothe him with purpose.

7. The Burning Bush — When God Reintroduces Purpose

In Midian, God appeared to Moses in a burning bush:

"I have surely seen the oppression of My people...

So, I have come down to deliver them."

(Exodus 3:7–8)

But God doesn't come down without sending a man.

The moment God said, "I am come down,"

He followed with:

"Come now, therefore, and I will send you..."

(Exodus 3:10)

This moment was spiritual ordination.

God was reappointing Moses to what Satan tried to destroy.

8. Moses Returns to Egypt — Confronting the Kingdom of Darkness

When Moses returned to Egypt,

he was no longer a fugitive —

he was a deliverer.

Every miracle God performed through Moses

was a judgment on the gods of Egypt.

- water turned to blood
- frogs
- lice
- flies
- livestock disease
- boils
- hail
- locusts
- darkness
- death of the firstborn

Each plague was not random —

each was a strike against a demonic principality.

God was dismantling the spiritual power structure behind Egypt.

9. The Red Sea — When Hell Thought It Had Israel Trapped

Israel stood trapped:

- mountains on the left
- desert on the right
- Red Sea in front
- Pharaoh's army behind

It looked like the final defeat.

But then…

"Stand still and see the salvation of the LORD."

(Exodus 14:13)

God parted the sea.

Israel walked through on dry ground.

The waters destroyed Pharaoh's army.

The place where the enemy thought Israel would die

became the place of Israel's greatest deliverance.

This is always the pattern:

The enemy sets the trap —

but God sets the victory.

10. The Message of Moses' Life

Moses teaches us:

- Great destinies attract deadly attacks
- The enemy fears who you will become
- Satan attacks infancy because he fears maturity
- God hides His chosen ones in unexpected places
- Your worst failures cannot cancel your calling
- God prepares you in the wilderness
- Miracles are weapons in spiritual warfare
- When God fights for you, no enemy can stand
- And God ALWAYS finishes what He starts

Ultimately:

The battle is spiritual —

but God won the end from the beginning.

CHAPTER SEVEN: DAVID: ANOINTED, ATTACKED, AND PRESERVED

"The LORD who delivered me… He will deliver me." — 1 Samuel 17:37 (NKJV)

Whenever God anoints a person,

hell assigns an adversary.

David's life reveals a profound truth:

The anointing attracts warfare.

Destiny draws opposition.

Purpose provokes the enemy.

The moment God placed His hand on David,

Satan unleashed attack after attack

to stop him from reaching the throne

through which the Messiah would one day come.

1. The Anointing: When God Marks You, Hell Sees It

David was chosen by God while hidden in a field.

He wasn't voted in.

He wasn't selected by men.

He wasn't positioned by family.

God chose him.

When Samuel poured the oil,

three things happened instantly:

- the Spirit of the Lord came upon David (1 Samuel 16:13)
- the Spirit departed from Saul
- an evil spirit began tormenting Saul (v. 14)

This was not coincidence —

it was spiritual warfare.

The moment David was anointed,

the battle for the throne began.

Satan knew:

If David sits on the throne,

then the lineage to Christ remains unbroken.

So, the enemy stirred opposition through Saul.

2. Goliath — The First Giant Meant to Destroy David's Destiny

Goliath was more than a champion —

he was a demonic intimidation sent to stop the next move of God.

Goliath's purpose was clear:

- to paralyze Israel
- to break their faith
- to destroy their courage
- To prevent David's emergence

David's battle with Goliath was not random —

it was prophetic.

Goliath stood in David's way

because David was standing in the way of darkness.

But God gave David supernatural courage:

"I come to you in the name of the LORD of hosts."

(1 Samuel 17:45)

One stone became a divine weapon.

One sling became an act of faith.

One boy became a deliverer.

Goliath fell —

and David's destiny rose.

3. Saul's Jealousy — A Demonically Inspired Hatred

After David killed Goliath, the women sang:

"Saul has slain his thousands,

and David his ten thousands."

(1 Samuel 18:7)

This song opened a spiritual door.

Saul became filled with jealousy—

the same spiritual poison Cain felt toward Abel.

Jealousy is always a sign

that the enemy fears your destiny.

The Bible says:

"Saul eyed David from that day forward."

(1 Samuel 18:9)

A demonic spirit entered Saul

and turned him into an enemy of David's calling.

This was satanic manipulation:

- attempt to kill David with a spear
- sending him into dangerous battles
- using his own daughter to trap him
- mobilizing armies to hunt him

Saul became an instrument in the enemy's hand.

But David was wrapped in God's promise.

4. Rejection from His Own People — When God Uses Opposition as Direction

David ran for his life.

He hid in caves.

He was hunted like an animal.

He was rejected by Israel and misunderstood by friends.

This was not coincidence —

it was divine direction.

Every rejection pushed David toward the throne.

Every betrayal pushed him deeper into God.

Every attack shaped his heart into a king.

What the enemy meant to crush him,

God used to train him.

5. Jonathan — God Sends Covenant Helpers in Seasons of Attack

In the middle of the warfare,

God raised Jonathan as a covenant friend.

Jonathan:

- protected David
- warned David
- strengthened David

- affirmed David's destiny
- loved David like a brother
- helped preserve the future king

This reveals a principle:

When hell rises against you,

God sends people who carry His heart.

Jonathan was heaven's answer to Saul's hatred.

6. The Wilderness Years — When God Shapes Kings in Secret

David's wilderness years were not punishment —

they were preparation.

In the wilderness David learned:

- humility
- dependency on God
- leadership
- worship
- warfare
- Patience
- mercy
- wisdom
- Submission

God molds His warriors in private

before He reveals them in public.

David's character was forged

in caves, deserts, and hidden places.

And even in hiding,

God preserved David:

- Saul came inches from killing him
- enemies ambushed him
- armies searched for him
- spies tracked him
- betrayers revealed his location

Yet every time:

BUT GOD delivered David.

7. David Spares Saul — Victory Over the Spirit Behind the Man

Twice David had the chance to kill Saul.

Twice he refused.

Because David understood something profound:

The real enemy was not Saul

— it was the spirit influencing him.

David fought the war

without touching the man.

This is why God said David was

"a man after My own heart."

David did not fight for the throne

by force or manipulation —

he waited on God's timing.

This is the sign of a man who trusts God

more than opportunity.

8. The Throne — God Fulfills the Promise Hell Tried to Block

After years of trials,

David became king.

- First over Judah
- Then over all Israel

The throne was secured.

The covenant was established.

The lineage was protected.

And God made a prophetic promise:

"Your house and your kingdom shall be established forever...

Your throne shall be established forever."

(2 Samuel 7:16)

This was not about David alone —

it was about Christ,

the Son of David,

the Lion of the Tribe of Judah.

Satan tried everything to stop David,

but God's purpose prevailed.

9. David's Legacy — A Lineage the Enemy Could Not Destroy

David's line would produce:

- Solomon
- Kings of Judah
- Zerubbabel
- Joseph
- Mary
- JESUS

This is why the enemy fought David so violently.

But no attack could break the covenant.

Because God had declared it before time began.

10. The Message of David's Life

David's journey teaches us:

- The anointing attracts warfare
- Jealousy is a sign of spiritual threat
- Giants rise when destiny rises
- The enemy uses familiar people to attack purpose

- God uses rejection to reposition you
- Wilderness seasons shape kings
- God always sends helpers of destiny
- Your heart matters more than your crown
- What God promises, He preserves

And ultimately:

The battle is spiritual —

but God won the end from the beginning

CHAPTER EIGHT: ELIJAH VS. JEZEBEL: WHEN DARKNESS CONFRONTS LIGHT

"The God who answers by fire, He is God." — 1 Kings 18:24 (NKJV)

Every generation faces a Jezebel.

Every generation faces a spirit that rises to silence the prophetic voice,

destroy the altars of God,

and exalt the altars of darkness.

In Elijah's day,

Jezebel was not merely a queen —

she was the embodiment of a demonic principality,

a spiritual power sent to:

- Corrupt a nation
- Silence prophets
- kill the righteous
- replace God's worship with Baal
- and derail the destiny of Israel

In the midst of that darkness,

God raised one man — Elijah — the prophet of fire.

His story reveals the power of one voice of obedience

against an entire kingdom of darkness.

1. The Rise of Jezebel — Satan's Weapon Against a Nation

Jezebel was not just a wicked woman —

she carried the spirit of witchcraft, manipulation, and idolatry.

When she married King Ahab:

- she imported Baal worship into Israel,
- slaughtered the prophets of the LORD,
- erected demonic altars,
- seduced the people into idolatry,
- and established spiritual dominance through fear.

This was not politics —

this was spiritual invasion.

Israel was a chosen nation.

From Israel would come the Messiah.

If Israel fell into idolatry,

the lineage would be endangered.

So, Satan used Jezebel to attack the purpose of God.

2. God Raises Elijah — A Voice to Confront Darkness

Elijah appears suddenly,

with no genealogy,

no introduction,

no background.

Why?

Because when darkness rises quickly,

God raises deliverers without delay.

Elijah declared:

"As the LORD God of Israel lives... there shall not be dew nor rain these years, except at my word."

(1 Kings 17:1)

This was not simply a drought —

it was a judgment against Baal,

the false god believed to control rain.

Elijah's words directly challenged the demonic power ruling Israel.

3. Divine Protection in Hiding — When Obedience Makes You a Target

After Elijah declared the drought, God said:

"Hide yourself..."

(1 Kings 17:3)

Why?

Because Jezebel had already begun killing the prophets.

Elijah was next on her list.

But God hid Elijah supernaturally:

- by a brook
- fed by ravens
- sustained by a widow
- protected every step

Elijah was hidden because Elijah was chosen.

God hides His vessels until the appointed time of confrontation.

4. Mount Carmel — The Battle Between Two Kingdoms

The drought broke Israel spiritually.

The people were torn between God and Baal.

Elijah declared the greatest spiritual showdown in the Old Testament:

"How long will you falter between two opinions?

If the LORD is God, follow Him;

but if Baal, follow him."

(1 Kings 18:21)

On Mount Carmel:

- 450 prophets of Baal
- 400 prophets of Asherah
- Jezebel's entire demonic system
- versus one prophet of God

This was not Elijah vs. Baal.

This was God vs. Satan.

Light vs. darkness.

Truth vs. deception.

Elijah allowed the prophets of Baal to call on their god:

- they cried
- they shouted
- they cut themselves
- they prophesied lies
- no fire fell

Because demons cannot answer prayer—

they only manipulate fear.

Then Elijah rebuilt the altar of the LORD —

the true battlefield.

When he prayed:

"Answer me, O LORD,

that this people may know that You are God..."

(1 Kings 18:37)

Fire fell from heaven.

Consuming the sacrifice, altar, stones, and water.

This was a spiritual message:

The God of Elijah is the God who answers by fire.

The God of Israel is the true God.

Jezebel cannot stop the purpose of God.

5. Jezebel Strikes Back — The Spirit of Intimidation

When Jezebel heard of Elijah's victory, she sent a message:

"So let the gods do to me... if I do not make your life as one of them by tomorrow."

(1 Kings 19:2)

Notice:

She didn't send soldiers.

She sent words.

Because Jezebel's true power is intimidation.

She fights the mind.

She targets courage.

She silences voices.

Satan could not defeat Elijah on the mountain,

so, he tried to defeat him in his thoughts.

Elijah fled —

not because he was weak,

but because the spirit of Jezebel carries supernatural intimidation.

This is why many gifted, called, anointed people

suddenly feel fear, depression, or despair

after great victories.

It is not emotional.

It is spiritual backlash.

6. Elijah Under the Juniper Tree — When the Battle Turns Inward

Elijah said:

"It is enough... take my life."

(1 Kings 19:4)

The same man who called fire down from heaven

now wanted to die.

This reveals something deep:

Spiritual battles can break even the strongest when the fight is prolonged.

But God did not condemn Elijah.

He refreshed him.

- An angel touched him
- Fed him supernatural food

- Strengthened his body
- Consolved his soul
- Revived his spirit

God knows when His warriors are tired.

And He provides heavenly strength.

7. God's Whisper — The Voice That Breaks Jezebel's Power

On Mount Horeb, God asked Elijah:

"What are you doing here?"

Elijah poured out his heart.

Then God said:

"Go, return..."

(1 Kings 19:15)

God recommissioned Elijah

because the battle was not over.

Then God revealed something that killed Jezebel's intimidation:

"I have seven thousand in Israel...

who have not bowed to Baal."

(1 Kings 19:18)

Elijah thought he was alone.

But God always has a remnant.

The spirit of Jezebel is defeated

when you understand you are not alone.

8. Jezebel's End — The Prophet God Raised to Finish the Battle

Elijah's assignment ended,

but the war did not.

God raised Jehu —

a warrior with prophetic anointing —

to confront Jezebel.

Her death was exactly as God foretold:

"The dogs shall eat Jezebel..."

(1 Kings 21:23)

The woman who threatened God's prophet

died under God's judgment.

Because:

Every Jezebel will fall.

Every demonic system will collapse.

Every attack on God's purpose will fail.

9. The Message of Elijah's Battle

Elijah's story teaches us:

- When darkness rises, God raises a voice
- Prophetic assignments attract demonic opposition

- Intimidation is Satan's favorite weapon
- Every Jezebel spirit seeks to silence the prophetic
- God hides His servants until the right moment
- Every altar built against you will be exposed by fire
- God strengthens His warriors when they are weary
- No Jezebel can stop a God-ordained destiny
- And every spiritual throne built by darkness will fall

Ultimately:

The battle is spiritual —

but God won the end from the beginning.

CHAPTER NINE: DANIEL: WHEN PRAYER SHAKES PRINCIPALITIES

"From the first day… your words were heard, and I have come because of your words." — Daniel 10:12 (NKJV)

Daniel's life opens the curtain of the spiritual realm

and reveals realities most believers never see.

In Daniel, we see:

- angels on assignment,
- demonic princes ruling regions,
- spiritual warfare affecting earthly kingdoms,
- divine revelation opposed by darkness,
- and prayer that moves heaven and shakes hell.

Daniel was not just a prophet —

he was a man whose faith disrupted the plans of darkness

and preserved the destiny of Israel

while they were exiled in Babylon.

1. Israel in Babylon — A Nation Under Spiritual Attack

Babylon was more than a place of exile —

it was a satanic empire built on:

- witchcraft,
- idols,
- astrology,
- sorcery,
- demonic influence,
- and rebellion against God.

For Satan, Babylon was the perfect environment

to destroy Israel's identity

and prevent the restoration of the nation

through which the Messiah would come.

So, the enemy used Babylon to:

- rename them,
- re-educate them,
- reshape their identity,

- erase their worship,
- and disconnect them from God.

But God raised Daniel

— a man who refused to bow.

2. Daniel's Resolve — The Power of a Consecrated Heart

Daniel made a decision:

"Daniel purposed in his heart..."

(Daniel 1:8)

This one decision:

- shut the door to compromise,
- broke the power of Babylon over him,
- set him apart for God's use,
- and prepared him for divine revelation.

Satan attacks the heart first

because a defiled heart cannot see clearly

or stand boldly.

But Daniel's consecration

became his greatest weapon.

3. The King's Dream — Satan's Attempt to Kill an Entire Generation

Nebuchadnezzar demanded that the wise men

tell both the dream and the interpretation

(Daniel 2).

If they could not,

he commanded all wise men be killed.

This included Daniel and his friends.

This was more than royal anger —

it was a demonic plan to:

- eliminate the prophetic voice,
- remove God's chosen vessels,
- and silence divine revelation.

But Daniel prayed.

And God revealed the dream in the night.

What Satan intended as execution,

God used as elevation.

Daniel was at once promoted —

a strategic move that positioned him

to influence the most powerful empire on earth.

4. The Fiery Furnace — When Worship Becomes Warfare

Shadrach, Meshach, and Abed-Nego

refused to worship the golden image.

This was not simply a statue —

it was a demonic portal of worship

designed to steal glory from God

and commit a nation to idolatry.

Their refusal triggered Satan's fury:

- the furnace was heated seven times hotter,
- the strongest soldiers bound them,
- and the king prepared their execution.

But then…

BUT GOD stepped into the fire.

A fourth man appeared—

one like the Son of God.

What was meant to kill them

became the platform for God's glory.

The fire burned the ropes,

but not their bodies.

The flame released them

instead of consuming them.

When you belong to God,

fire becomes freedom.

5. Daniel in the Lions' Den — Satan's Plan to Silence the Prophet

Daniel's enemies manipulated the law

to trap him through his own prayer life.

They knew:

- Daniel would rather die than stop praying,
- his devotion made him unstoppable,
- and his influence threatened darkness.

The decree was demonic:

"Anyone who prays to any god except you shall be cast into the den of lions."

This was a direct attack on Daniel's spiritual power

and a coordinated plan to kill him.

But Daniel continued praying —

windows open,

face toward Jerusalem,

heart fixed on God.

He refused to hide his devotion.

Daniel was thrown into the lions' den.

But heaven went with him.

God sent His angel

to shut the lions' mouths.

The predators that should have devoured him

became pillows under him.

6. The Vision of Spiritual Warfare — When the Prince of

Persia Resisted

Daniel prayed for 21 days,

seeking revelation from God.

On the 21st day,

an angel appeared.

He said:

"From the first day... your words were heard..."

"...but the prince of Persia withstood me 21 days."

(Daniel 10:12–13)

This is one of the clearest revelations

of how spiritual warfare affects answers to prayer.

Notice:

1. Heaven heard immediately

God does not delay.

Demonic resistance does.

2. A demonic principality resisted a heavenly messenger

The "prince of Persia" was not a human king

but a territorial demon over the Persian empire.

3. The battle lasted 21 days

Not because God was weak,

but because the enemy fought intensely

to prevent Daniel from receiving revelation

that would shape Israel's future.

4. Michael, the archangel, entered the battle

When warfare escalates,

God sends higher-ranking angels.

Your prayer mobilizes heaven.

7. Revelation Released — God Overrules Darkness

When the angel finally reached Daniel,

he brought:

- prophetic insight,
- revelation of the future kingdoms,
- clarity about Israel's destiny,
- insight regarding spiritual warfare,
- and messages that affect even our generation.

The enemy fought to block these revelations

because they expose his strategies

and reveal God's victorious plan.

But he could not stop the angel.

He could not stop the message.

He could not stop God's purpose.

8. Daniel's Impact — A Man Who Shaped Nations

Through Prayer

Daniel's life proves:

- prayer changes nations,
- prayer breaks demonic influence,
- prayer opens seals of revelation,
- prayer moves angels,
- and prayer causes heaven to intervene.

Daniel never carried a sword,

never led an army,

never fought a physical battle.

Yet he overthrew kingdoms through prayer

and shook hell through intimacy with God.

He was a prophet to kings

and a terror to demons.

9. The Message of Daniel's Life

Daniel shows us that:

- Satan assigns principalities to resist God's purpose
- Prayer is a weapon that pierces darkness
- Fasting weakens demonic influence
- God sends angels in response to prayer
- Demons can delay but cannot defeat divine answers

- Integrity protects your spiritual authority
- Faithfulness keeps you unshaken in trials
- The power of God is stronger than the laws of men
- Divine revelation is a threat to demonic kingdoms
- And no den of lions can stop the will of God

Ultimately:

The battle is spiritual —

but God won the end from the beginning.

CHAPTER TEN: ESTHER: WHEN THE ENEMY PLOTS GENOCIDE BUT GOD TURNS THE TABLES

"For such a time as this." — Esther 4:14 (NKJV)

Behind every threat against God's people

is a strategy from the kingdom of darkness.

Behind every deliverance

is the sovereign hand of God.

The book of Esther pulls back the spiritual curtain

and reveals the invisible war to destroy the entire Jewish nation—

a nation chosen to bring forth the Messiah.

Satan's plan was not simply genocide.

It was an attempt to erase the lineage of Christ

and end God's redemptive plan.

But when the enemy plots destruction,

God positions deliverance.

1. Israel in Persia — A Nation Under Threat

After Babylon fell, the Persian Empire ruled.

Israel was scattered throughout the provinces.

The people were vulnerable:

no temple,

no walls,

no army,

no king,

and no apparent protection.

Satan saw an opportunity

to destroy the nation in one decisive blow.

So, the enemy raised a man.

2. Haman — A Vessel of Satan's Hatred

Haman was not simply an official in the Persian government.

He carried a generational hatred.

He was an Agagite—

descendant of King Agag,

whom God commanded Saul to utterly destroy (1 Sam. 15).

Saul's disobedience centuries earlier

left a door open for an enemy spirit

to rise again in Haman.

Haman carried:

- a murderous spirit,
- A genocidal assignment,
- a demonic hatred for the Jews,
- and pride fueled by hell.

When Mordecai refused to bow,

Haman's anger turned from one man

to the entire nation.

This was spiritual.

Satan wanted to wipe out all Jews at once—

including the line of Judah,

the line of David,

the line of Christ.

3. The Demonic Decree — The First Attempt to Destroy God's People Entirely

Haman convinced King Ahasuerus to issue a decree

stating that on a specific day

all Jews in every province

were to be:

- killed,
- plundered,
- and destroyed.

This was more than human hatred.

It was satanic strategy.

If the decree succeeded:

- the promise to Abraham would be broken,
- the covenant with David would collapse,
- the prophetic Scriptures would fail,
- and the Messiah would never come.

Satan believed he had finally found

a way to end God's plan.

But God was already moving.

4. God's Hidden Strategy — Esther on the Throne

God placed Esther in the palace

before Haman conceived his plan.

God always positions deliverance

before the enemy positions destruction.

Esther was:

- a Jewish orphan,
- raised by Mordecai,
- chosen among many,
- placed in favor,
- appointed for a purpose.

To everyone else,

she was simply a new queen.

To heaven,

she was the vessel of deliverance.

To hell,

she was a threat waiting to be activated.

5. Mordecai's Warning — When Purpose Is Summoned

When Mordecai told Esther of the decree,

she hesitated.

Approaching the king uninvited

meant death.

Fear rose.

Doubt rose.

Risk rose.

But Mordecai said words that thunder across generations:

> *"Who knows whether you have come to the kingdom*

for such a time as this?"

(Esther 4:14)

This was not coincidence.

This was calling.

Esther was born for this moment.

You know you're in purpose

when your assignment requires risk.

6. Esther's Decision — Fasting, Prayer, and Courage

Esther declared:

"If I perish, I perish!"

This was spiritual war.

She called a three-day fast—

not for beauty,

not for favor,

but for deliverance.

Fasting:

- weakens the enemy's influence,
- aligns the spirit with God,
- breaks fear,
- and opens doors that flesh cannot open.

Heaven responded.

The king extended his golden scepter—

a prophetic symbol of divine favor.

7. The Exposing of Haman — God Turns the Trap on the Enemy

Esther invited the king and Haman

to two private banquets.

Haman thought he was being honored.

In reality, he was being exposed.

At the second banquet, Esther revealed:

- the plot,
- the danger,
- her identity,
- and her request.

Suddenly, the king saw Haman

for whom he really was.

The evil he planned

returned on his own head.

The gallows Haman built for Mordecai

became the place of his own death.

This is how God fights:

He turns the enemy's weapons back on the enemy.

8. The Reversal — When God Overrules the Laws of Men

But the decree could not be reversed

— Persian law was permanent.

So, God gave Esther and Mordecai

wisdom for a second decree:

- enabling Israel to defend themselves,
- strike their enemies,
- and destroy those who sought their death.

The reversal was supernatural.

Instead of Israel being destroyed…

their enemies fell.

Instead of mourning…

they celebrated.

Instead of defeat…

they triumphed.

Instead of extinction…

they multiplied.

What Satan meant as genocide

became a holiday of victory — Purim.

9. The Preservation of the Messianic Lineage

The book of Esther reveals this truth:

God preserved Israel so He could preserve the Messiah.

Through Esther's obedience:

- the tribe of Judah survived,
- the line of David continued,
- the prophets remained,
- the covenant endured,
- and the Messiah's lineage was protected.

Satan lost.

God's plan marched forward.

10. The Message of Esther's Victory

Esther's story teaches us:

- Satan plans destruction long before it appears
- God positions deliverance long before it's needed
- Fear cannot stop a God-ordained assignment
- Fasting breaks the power of darkness
- God exposes hidden enemies
- What the enemy builds will destroy himself
- God can overturn any decree, system, or government
- One obedient vessel can save a nation
- And no plot of hell can stop the purpose of God

Ultimately:

The battle is spiritual —

but God won the end from the beginning.

CHAPTER ELEVEN: JOB: WHEN THE BATTLE TOUCHES YOUR LIFE BUT GOD SETS THE LIMITS

"You have hedged me behind and before and laid Your hand upon me." — Psalm 139:5 (NKJV)

Job's story is one of the most misunderstood spiritual battles in the Bible.

Many think it is a story of suffering.

But in truth, it is a story of divine sovereignty,

Satanic limitation,

Unshakeable faith,

and supernatural restoration.

Job reveals a foundational truth:

The enemy cannot touch your life unless God allows it,

and if God permits it, there is purpose in it.

Job is not the story of a man losing everything.

Job is the story of a man protected, tested, vindicated, and restored by God.

1. Job: A Man Marked by God Before the Battle Began

Job was:

- blameless
- upright
- a worshiper
- a family man
- a wealthy man
- a man who feared God
- a man who shunned evil

(Job 1:1–5)

He was favored by heaven

and targeted by hell.

The enemy notices those God favors.

He studies those who walk in righteousness.

He hates those who love God sincerely.

Job's devotion made him a threat to darkness.

2. The Heavenly Courtroom — The Real Battleground

The story begins not on earth,

but in heaven.

"The sons of God came to present themselves before the LORD,

and Satan also came among them."

(Job 1:6)

We learn four unchanging spiritual truths here:

1. Satan must report to God.

He is not equal to God.

He is a created being.

He is under divine authority.

2. Satan cannot act without permission.

He needs clearance to attack.

He cannot touch what God guards.

3. God initiated the conversation about Job.

God said:

"Have you considered My servant Job?"

(Job 1:8)

This means:

- God knew Job's faith
- God trusted Job's endurance

- God was about to elevate Job
- God was going to use Job to humiliate Satan

4. The battlefield was Job's righteousness.

Satan accused Job of serving God only because of blessing.

Satan hates true worship.

He hates pure motives.

He hates righteousness.

So, the enemy challenged Job's integrity in front of heaven.

3. Satan's Accusation — The Attack Must Be Allowed

The enemy said:

"Does Job fear God for nothing?"

(Job 1:9)

Then Satan attacked three areas:

1. Job's hedge:

He said:

"You have hedged him in."

(Job 1:10)

This reveals that God puts a spiritual hedge around His children.

2. Job's family and possessions:

Satan believed removing Job's blessings

would destroy Job's faith.

3. Job's health:

Satan believed that bodily suffering

would break Job's devotion.

But God set limits:

"Behold, all he has is in your power,

but do not lay a hand on his person."

(Job 1:12)

Satan can never go beyond the boundary God draws.

4. The Attack Begins — Satan Strikes Job's Life with Violence

In rapid succession:

- Sabeans stole Job's oxen
- Fire from heaven burned his sheep
- Chaldeans stole his camels
- A wind destroyed the house where his children were
- His servants died
- His wealth vanished
- His family was gone

These attacks were not natural events.

They were spiritual assaults executed through human and natural means.

But even after all this:

"In all this Job did not sin nor charge God with wrong."

(Job 1:22)

The enemy failed.

So, he asked for a second permission.

5. The Attack on the Body — Satan Strikes Job with Pain

God said:

"Behold, he is in your hand,

but spare his life."

(Job 2:6)

Satan cannot kill you.

Not when God has spoken life over you.

Job was afflicted with painful boils

from head to toe.

He sat in ashes, scraping his skin.

His wife urged him to curse God.

His friends accused him of hidden sin.

This was not just physical —

it was emotional, mental, and relational warfare.

The enemy attacked:

- his body,
- his reputation,

- his marriage,
- his faith,
- his dignity,
- his identity.

But even then…

"Though He slay me, yet will I trust Him."

(Job 13:15)

Job refused to let the devil define his God.

6. The Silence of God — The Hardest Part of the Battle

For 37 chapters,

God said nothing.

This silence was a test,

not abandonment.

God was watching:

- Job's worship
- Job's faith
- Job's endurance
- Job's integrity

Satan cannot understand a believer

who worships in silence.

7. God Speaks — When Heaven Breaks the Silence

Finally, God answered out of the whirlwind:

"Where were you when I laid the foundations of the earth?"

(Job 38:4)

God did not explain the suffering.

He revealed His sovereignty.

God lifted Job's eyes from the pain

to the majesty of His power.

When God reveals Himself,

the battle ends.

8. Job Vindicated — God Overrules Every Accusation

God rebuked Job's friends.

God defended Job's integrity.

God restored Job's reputation.

Then came the restoration:

"And the LORD restored Job's losses

when he prayed for his friends."

(Job 42:10)

This is divine justice:

- Job lost ten children — God gave him ten more
- Job lost wealth — God doubled it
- Job lost influence — God increased it

- Job lost dignity — God restored it fully
- Job lost nothing God could not replace

The enemy took from Job,

but God gave back more than the enemy could steal.

9. The Heavenly Verdict — Satan Shamed, Job Elevated

Job ended with:

- double blessing
- deeper revelation
- increased longevity
- restored honor
- divine approval

The unseen war ended with:

- Satan silenced
- Job vindicated
- God glorified
- future generations strengthened

10. The Message of Job's Life

Job teaches us that:

- God is always in control
- Satan must ask permission
- God sets the limits

- Suffering is a battleground, not a defeat
- True faith survives storms
- Silence is not abandonment
- God fights for His children
- God restores everything the enemy steals
- God turns the battle into a testimony
- And restoration is always greater than loss

Ultimately:

The battle is spiritual —

but God won the end from the beginning

CHAPTER TWELVE: THE BIRTH OF JESUS: THE SEED THE DRAGON COULD NOT DESTROY

"When the fullness of the time had come, God sent forth His Son…" — Galatians 4:4 (NKJV)

Before Jesus was born in Bethlehem,

hell was in full panic mode.

For thousands of years, Satan had been fighting one thing:

the promise of the Seed —

the One who would crush the serpent's head

and break the power of darkness forever.

Every attack in Scripture —

Cain and Abel,

Noah,

Abraham,

Isaac,

Jacob,

Judah,

David,

Israel —

was aiming to stop this moment.

The birth of Jesus Christ

was the ultimate clash between the kingdom of darkness

and the kingdom of God.

1. The Fullness of Time — Heaven Moves, Hell Reacts

When Jesus was conceived,

heaven moved and hell reacted.

Jesus did not appear randomly.

He came:

- at the right time,
- in the right place,
- under the right empire,
- according to prophecy,

- through the right lineage,
- by divine appointment.

Every prophecy converged perfectly:

- Born of a woman (Genesis 3:15)
- Born in Bethlehem (Micah 5:2)
- Born of a virgin (Isaiah 7:14)
- From the tribe of Judah (Genesis 49:10)
- From the line of David (2 Samuel 7:16)

God was fulfilling thousands of years of promise.

And Satan knew it.

2. The War in the Womb — The Dragon Waits for the Child

Revelation 12 reveals the unseen dimension:

"The dragon stood before the woman who was ready to give birth,

to devour her Child as soon as it was born."

(Revelation 12 :4)

This was not metaphor —

it was spiritual reality.

Satan was waiting to destroy Jesus

the moment He entered the world.

Because the Seed in Mary's womb

was the death sentence of Satan.

And so, the war intensified.

3. Mary and Joseph — Chosen, Attacked, and Protected

Mary was chosen—

pure, favored, surrendered.

But with calling came warfare.

Satan attacked:

1. Her reputation

Accusations of immorality.

Whispers.

Stigma.

A scandal in Nazareth.

2. Joseph's faith

Confusion, fear, doubt.

But God intervened through dreams.

3. Their unity

Satan tried to divide them

before Jesus was born.

But God sent an angel.

Wherever God birth's purpose,

He sends divine reassurance.

4. Herod — Satan's Instrument of Mass Murder

When the wise men inquired about the King of the Jews,

Herod was troubled—

and behind Herod was hell.

The same spirit drove herod

that drove Pharaoh in Moses' day:

Destroy the deliverer before He rises.

So, Herod ordered the massacre

of all male children two years old and under

(Matthew 2:16).

This was not politics.

It was demonic genocide.

Hell was trying to kill the Messiah

in His infancy.

But then…

BUT GOD intervened.

An angel appeared to Joseph:

"Arise… flee to Egypt…

for Herod will seek the young Child to destroy Him."

(Matthew 2:13)

God protected Jesus by sending Him to Egypt —

the same nation that once tried to kill deliverers.

God often hides His greatest purposes

in the very places the enemy used for destruction.

Herod failed.

Satan failed.

The Seed lived.

5. Bethlehem — God's Sovereignty Over Every Detail

Jesus was born in Bethlehem

because Caesar Augustus issued a census.

A pagan emperor —

moved by God —

fulfilled prophecy.

This reveals:

- The enemy does not control history
- Humans do not control prophecy
- God directs the hearts of kings
- Everything happens "in the fullness of time"

No attack could stop Jesus from being born

exactly where God ordained.

6. The Shepherds and Angels — Heaven Announces Victory

The night Jesus was born,

heaven exploded with angelic praise.

Why?

Because the Seed had arrived.

The One foretold since Eden.

The One the prophets saw from afar.

The One the angels longed to understand.

The dragon failed.

The Messiah was here.

7. Simeon and Anna — Prophetic Witnesses

When Jesus was brought to the temple:

- Simeon prophesied His destiny,
- Anna confirmed His identity.

Two elderly prophets

bearing witness to the newborn King.

God always confirms His purpose

in the presence of witnesses.

8. Jesus Hidden in Nazareth — God Protects Destiny in Obscurity

After Herod died,

Joseph moved the family to Nazareth.

This fulfilled prophecy:

"He shall be called a Nazarene."

(Matthew 2:23)

Nazareth was the last place Satan would expect the Messiah to be raised.

God hid Jesus in a place

of no reputation,

no influence,

no significance.

Because God hides His greatest purpose

in humility.

9. Why Satan Could Not Destroy the Seed

Satan failed because:

- God protected every detail
- God sent angels on assignment
- God guided Joseph supernaturally
- God positioned the right people
- God moved kings and kingdoms
- God hid Jesus at the right time
- God revealed Him at the right time
- And prophecy was stronger than warfare

The enemy tried to:

- corrupt the lineage

- Destroy Israel
- slaughter infants
- manipulate kings
- stir fear
- whisper lies
- bring confusion
- create turmoil

But nothing could stop Him.

Jesus came.

Jesus lived.

Jesus conquered.

10. The Message of Jesus' Birth

The birth of Christ proves:

- God's plan cannot be stopped,
- prophecy prevails over attack,
- angels guard divine purpose,
- the timing of God is perfect,
- and Satan's power is limited.

Every attempt to stop Him failed.

Ultimately:

The battle is spiritual —

but God won the end from the beginning.

CHAPTER THIRTEEN: THE MINISTRY OF JESUS: WHEN LIGHT CONFRONTS DARKNESS

"For this purpose, the Son of God was manifested, that He might destroy the works of the devil." — 1 John 3:8 (NKJV)

When Jesus stepped into public ministry at age thirty,

He did not merely begin teaching, healing, or performing miracles.

He declared war.

The Light walked onto the battlefield.

The King entered enemy territory.

The Seed promised in Eden finally revealed Himself openly.

For thousands of years the enemy fought the lineage—

but now he had to face the Person.

From the moment Jesus appeared,

hell trembled.

Because Jesus did not simply oppose darkness…

He dismantled it.

1. The Voice in the Wilderness — Preparing the Battlefront

Before Jesus appeared publicly,

God raised John the Baptist.

John was:

- a voice in the wilderness,
- a breaker anointing,
- a prophetic alarm,
- a spiritual bulldozer clearing the path.

John's message :

"Prepare the way of the LORD."

(Isaiah 40:3)

This announcement shook the unseen realm.

The Messiah was stepping into His assignment.

The war was about to begin.

2. The Baptism — Heaven Opens, Hell Reacts

When Jesus was baptized:

- The heavens opened
- The Spirit descended like a dove
- The Father spoke audibly
- The Son was revealed

This is one of the greatest spiritual moments in human history.

The Trinity revealed themselves publicly,

declaring:

"THIS IS MY BELOVED SON."

Hell heard it too.

And immediately after…

3. The Wilderness Temptation — Satan's Direct Confrontation

The Spirit led Jesus into the wilderness

—not to be defeated,

but to defeat Satan publicly.

Satan used three strategies:

1. Attack the flesh

"Turn stones into bread."

2. Attack the mind

"Throw Yourself down… God will catch You."

3. Attack the spirit

"Bow to me and I'll give You the kingdoms."

These were not random temptations.

They were the same weapons Satan used on Adam:

- appetite
- pride
- power

But this time, Satan failed.

Every attack was met with:

"It is written."

Jesus defeated Satan in the wilderness

before defeating him at the Cross.

The second Adam succeeded

where the first Adam failed.

4. The Synagogue Showdown — Demons Exposed in Public

When Jesus preached in Capernaum,

a demon possessed man manifested and screamed:

"I know who You are—

the Holy One of God!"

(Luke 4:34)

Demons could hide from men.

But they could not hide from Jesus.

Everywhere He went:

- demons cried out
- Spirits trembled
- strongholds shattered
- darkness screamed in pain

Because the Light had entered the room.

Jesus cast the demon out with one sentence:

"Be quiet and come out of him!"

No ritual.

No incantation.

No struggle.

Just authority.

5. Healing the Sick — Destroying the Works of Darkness

Every sickness Jesus healed

was a victory over Satanic oppression.

Scripture says:

"...He healed all who were oppressed by the devil..."

(Acts 10:38)

This means:

- diseases,
- infirmities,
- paralysis,
- blindness,
- deafness,
- fevers,
- and torments

were manifestations of spiritual bondage.

When Jesus healed,

He wasn't just restoring bodies.

He was overthrowing demonic tyrannies.

Every miracle was a battle won.

6. Storms, Winds, and Waves — Creation Recognizes Its Master

When Jesus slept in the boat,

a violent storm arose.

This storm was not natural.

It was demonic.

Jesus rebuked the wind and sea

the same way He rebuked demons

(Mark 4:39).

Creation obeyed.

Disciples trembled.

Hell realized:

"Even the winds and the waves obey Him."

The Creator was walking in creation.

And creation recognized His voice.

7. The Legion of Demons — A Full-Scale Demonic Assault

In the region of the Gadarenes,

Jesus confronted a man possessed by a legion of demons

(6,000+).

The demons begged:

- "Don't torment us"
- "Don't send us to the abyss"
- "Let us enter the pigs"

They knew:

- Jesus was Judge
- Jesus was Sovereign
- Jesus held authority over their fate

He cast them out with a word.

An entire region was delivered

because one man was set free.

8. The Pharisees — Human Vessels Opposed to God's Purpose

The greatest human opposition Jesus faced

was not from sinners or Gentiles,

but from religious leaders.

The Pharisees:

- accused Him,
- plotted against Him,
- slandered Him,
- watched Him,
- tested Him,
- hated Him,
- sought to trap Him.

Behind them was a spirit—

the same religious spirit

that fights every move of God.

Satan used:

- Tradition,
- pride,
- hypocrisy,
- deception

to resist Jesus.

But every trap failed.

Every argument collapsed.

Every accusation exposed them.

9. Judas — Satan Enters a Vessel

When the time came for betrayal:

"Satan entered Judas."

(Luke 22:3)

This was not mere betrayal.

This was demonic possession.

Judas became the doorway

through which Satan attempted his final strike

against Jesus.

But what Satan meant as destruction

became the path to redemption.

10. The Ministry of Jesus — A Catalogue of Destroyed Darkness

Throughout His ministry, Jesus:

- healed lepers
- raised the dead
- opened blind eyes

- cleansed the temple
- preached the Kingdom
- cast out demons
- exposed hypocrisy
- rebuked storms
- forgave sins
- broke curses
- restored dignity
- declared truth
- revealed the Father
- demonstrated heaven on earth

Every act of Jesus was a blow to Satan's kingdom.

Jesus didn't come merely to preach—

He came to destroy.

Destroy sickness.

Destroy oppression.

Destroy deception.

Destroy sin.

Destroy death.

Destroy the works of the devil.

11. Why Darkness Could Not Stop Him

Darkness failed because:

- Jesus walked in perfect obedience
- Jesus walked in the power of the Spirit
- Jesus walked in kingdom authority
- Jesus worked in unbroken fellowship with the Father
- Every prophecy was on schedule
- Every step was divinely orchestrated
- Satan was outmatched, outpowered, outmaneuvered

The Light shined in darkness…

"... and the darkness did not overcome it."

(John 1:5)

12. The Message of Jesus' Ministry

Jesus' earthly ministry reveals:

- Darkness cannot resist light
- Demons submit to authority
- Sickness bows to the Word
- Nature obeys the Creator
- Satan recognizes Jesus' supremacy
- Religion opposes truth but cannot stop it
- Jesus is Lord over every realm—spiritual, natural, and eternal

Ultimately:

The battle is spiritual —

but God won the end from the beginning.

CHAPTER FOURTEEN: THE CROSS: WHEN DARKNESS THOUGHT IT WON… BUT GOD

"Having disarmed principalities and powers, He made a public spectacle of them, triumphing over them in it." — Colossians 2:15 (NKJV)

From the moment Jesus was born,

hell was terrified of Him.

But when Jesus entered His final hours,

all the forces of darkness

rose up in their fullest strength.

The Cross was not just a physical execution.

It was the climax of the invisible war

between the kingdom of darkness

and the kingdom of God.

Satan believed this was his moment of triumph.

But the Cross became the moment of his eternal defeat.

1. The Invisible War Intensifies — Gethsemane

Before Jesus was arrested,

He entered the Garden of Gethsemane—

the same kind of place

where the first Adam fell,

but where the last Adam would conquer.

Jesus said:

"My soul is exceedingly sorrowful, even to death."

(Mark 14:34)

This was not human fear.

It was spiritual warfare.

Hell was pressing in.

The weight of sin was descending.

The cup of judgment was before Him.

Satan attacked:

- His soul,
- His will,

- His emotions,
- His humanity.

But Jesus triumphed where Adam failed.

He prayed:

"Not My will, but Yours be done."

This was the victory of obedience

before the victory of the Cross.

2. Judas — Satan's Final Tool

Scripture says:

"Satan entered Judas..."

(Luke 22:3)

Judas was chosen by Jesus,

but captured by the enemy.

The betrayal was spiritual.

The kiss was demonic.

The plan was hell's design.

Yet Jesus called Judas:

"Friend."

Because Jesus knew—

even betrayal is part of the path to destiny.

3. The Arrest — Demonic Forces at Work

When the soldiers came,

Jesus said:

"This is your hour,

and the power of darkness."

(Luke 22:53)

This means:

- demons were present,
- darkness was active,
- the unseen realm was engaged.

The entire arrest was a satanic operation

allowed by God for a higher purpose.

4. The Trials — Hell Manipulates Human Systems

Jesus faced:

- false witnesses,
- corrupt leaders,
- manipulated crowds,
- political pressure,
- religious hatred,
- demonic influence.

Satan stirred the religious leaders.

The crowds were blinded by darkness.

Pilate was pressured by fear.

Every earthly structure

became a puppet of the unseen realm.

Hell believed it finally had the upper hand.

5. The Scourging — The Attack on the Body of the Savior

Roman scourging was brutal.

But the spiritual reality was far greater.

With every stripe:

- sickness was broken,
- infirmity was judged,
- curses were lifted,
- healing was purchased.

Isaiah prophesied:

"By His stripes we are healed."

(Isaiah 53:5)

What looked like defeat

was deliverance.

6. The Crown of Thorns — The Curse Broken

Thorns represent the curse of the ground

from Genesis 3:18.

By wearing a crown of thorns,

Jesus placed the curse upon His own head.

He became the curse

so, we could become the righteousness of God.

Every thorn was a declaration:

"The curse ends here."

7. Carrying the Cross — The Lamb on His Way to the Altar

As Jesus carried His Cross,

Hell rejoiced.

Demons whispered:

"He is weak."

"He is broken."

"He is defeated."

But in heaven's eyes,

He was ascending the hill of victory

to destroy the works of the devil.

The Lamb was walking toward redemption.

8. Golgotha — The Battlefield of Eternity

On the hill called "the place of the skull,"

the greatest war ever fought reached its peak.

They nailed His hands—

the hands that healed multitudes.

They nailed His feet—

the feet that carried the Gospel.

They lifted Him up—

the One who came from heaven.

The mocking,

the insults,

the darkness,

the agony—

all were part of the spiritual assault.

Hell believed:

"This is victory."

But it was their greatest mistake.

9. The Darkness from Noon to Three — The Father Judges Sin

For three hours,

darkness covered the land.

This was not weather.

It was judgment.

Jesus bore:

- the sin of the world,

- the wrath of God,
- the condemnation of humanity.

He became sin

so, we could become righteous.

He was forsaken

so, we could be accepted.

He suffered

so, we could be saved.

10. His Final Words — The Victory Cry

As His mission reached its completion,

Jesus cried out:

"It is finished!"

(John 19:30)

This was not a cry of defeat—

it was a cry of triumph.

"Finished" means:

- the debt is paid,
- the curse is broken,
- the prophecy fulfilled,
- the enemy defeated,
- salvation accomplished,

- the power of darkness dismantled.

Then He bowed His head

and gave up His spirit.

Jesus did not die—

He gave His life.

Darkness thought it had won.

But heaven smiled.

11. The Earthquake — Creation Responds to the Victory

When Jesus died:

- the earth shook,
- rocks split,
- the veil tore from top to bottom,
- tombs opened,
- the way into the Holy of Holies was revealed.

Creation could not remain silent.

Heaven declared:

"The sacrifice has been accepted."

12. The Enemy Defeated — The Triumph in the Spirit Realm

While His body lay in the tomb,

Jesus entered the realm of the dead

—not as a victim,

but as a conqueror.

He:

- stripped Satan of authority,
- took the keys of death and hell,
- broke the chains of captivity,
- proclaimed victory to the spirits in prison.

Colossians 2:15 says:

"He disarmed principalities and powers…"

Jesus didn't just defeat demons—

He disarmed them.

He exposed them.

He shamed them.

He paraded them in defeat.

Hell was overthrown

from the inside out.

13. The Message of the Cross

The Cross reveals:

- God's love is unstoppable
- Satan's power is limited
- Sin's dominion is broken

- Redemption is complete
- Prophecy is fulfilled
- Judgment is satisfied
- Mercy overflows
- Darkness cannot defeat light
- Death cannot hold the Author of life
- Hell cannot win against heaven

Ultimately:

The battle is spiritual —

but God won the end from the beginning.

CHAPTER FIFTEEN: THE RESURRECTION: WHEN THE STONE COULD NOT HOLD THE SAVIOR

"He is not here; for He is risen, as He said." — Matthew 28:6 (NKJV)

The Cross was the battlefield.

The Resurrection is the victory.

Satan bruised His heel,

but Jesus crushed the serpent's head.

For three days,

hell celebrated what it thought was a permanent victory.

Demons rejoiced.

Darkness laughed.

The grave closed its mouth in confidence.

But early on the third day,

everything changed in a moment that shook the universe.

What humanity saw as a closed tomb,

heaven saw as a ticking clock.

When the appointed moment arrived,

hell discovered this eternal truth:

You can seal the tomb,

but you cannot stop the resurrection.

1. The Watchers at the Tomb — Hell's Last Attempt to Prevent the Inevitable

After Jesus died,

the chief priests went to Pilate and said:

"That deceiver said, 'After three days I will rise.'"

(Matthew 27:63)

They feared His resurrection

more than His life.

So, they requested:

- a Roman seal,
- a guarded tomb,
- armed soldiers.

This wasn't just human fear —

it was demonic strategy.

Satan knew:

If Jesus rises, the war is over.

But you cannot guard against God.

You cannot seal against prophecy.

You cannot lock out the Creator of life.

2. Jesus in the Tomb — The Silent Victory

While His body lay still,

Jesus was not asleep.

He descended into the lower parts of the earth

(Ephesians 4:9).

There, He:

- proclaimed His victory,
- liberated captives,
- took the keys of death and Hades,
- and stripped Satan of authority.

Hell was invaded

by the One it tried to defeat.

The grave was vandalized

by the King it tried to imprison.

The tomb became the resting place

of a Conqueror, not a victim.

3. The Earthquake and the Angel — Heaven Invades the Tomb

On the third day,

a massive earthquake shook the ground.

An angel of the Lord descended:

- his appearance like lightning,
- his clothing white as snow.

He rolled back the stone—

not to let Jesus out,

but to let witnesses in.

The soldiers shook,

fell as dead men,

and fled in terror.

Darkness cannot stand in the presence of glory.

4. The Empty Tomb — Proof That Hell Lost Permanently

The angel declared to the women:

"He is not here; for He is risen."

These words annihilated:

- fear,

- doubt,
- sin,
- death,
- hell's dominion,
- Satan's plans,
- and every weapon of darkness.

The tomb was empty—

not by accident,

but by divine decree.

The One who created life

could not be held by death.

5. Jesus Appears — Victory Revealed to His Followers

Jesus appeared to:

- Mary Magdalene
- Peter
- The disciples
- The two on the road to Emmaus
- Over 500 brethren at once
- Thomas
- And many others

Every appearance was a declaration:

"I am alive."

Jesus didn't ascend immediately

because He wanted His followers to know:

- the battle is won,
- the curse is broken,
- the prophecy is fulfilled,
- the enemy is defeated,
- the Savior is eternal.

His presence restored broken hearts,

rekindled hope,

and ignited faith.

6. The Resurrection Body — The Firstborn of a New Creation

Jesus rose with:

- a glorified body,
- incorruptible life,
- unbreakable power,
- heavenly authority.

He walked through walls,

ate food with His disciples,

and ascended into heaven.

He became:

"The firstborn from the dead."

(Colossians 1:18)

His resurrection guarantees ours.

Death is no longer the end—

It is a doorway.

7. The Defeat of Death — The Last Enemy Falls

Death once reigned as the undefeated king.

But Jesus shattered its power.

Scripture declares:

"Death is swallowed up in victory."

(1 Corinthians 15:54)

Jesus not only died—

He conquered.

He not only conquered—

He reigns forever.

Death could not hold Him

because He is Life itself.

8. Satan's Final Defeat — The War Ends at the Empty Tomb

At the tomb:

- the devil lost his authority,

- death lost its sting,
- sin lost its power,
- hell lost its captives,
- the grave lost its victory.

The resurrection is the ultimate:

- answer to darkness,
- crushing of satanic power,
- triumph over evil,
- proof of divine sovereignty,
- manifestation of God's unstoppable purpose.

Satan fought for thousands of years

to prevent this moment.

But he failed.

BUT GOD raised Him from the dead.

9. The Great Commission — Passing the Victory to Believers

Before ascending, Jesus said:

"All authority has been given to Me in heaven and on earth."

(Matthew 28:18)

Then He delegated that authority to His disciples:

"Go therefore..."

The same authority Jesus used

to cast out demons,

heal the sick,

and preach the Kingdom

now rests upon His Church.

We do not fight for victory—

we fight from victory.

10. The Message of the Resurrection

The resurrection declares:

- God's plan cannot be stopped
- The enemy cannot overcome prophecy
- Jesus is Lord of heaven and earth
- The grave is defeated
- Death is temporary
- Satan is crushed
- Salvation is secure
- Hope is eternal
- Light triumphs over darkness
- And God's purpose is unstoppable

Ultimately:

The battle is spiritual —

but God won the end from the beginning.

CHAPTER SIXTEEN: THE CHURCH: EMPOWERED BY THE HOLY SPIRIT TO CONTINUE THE WAR AGAINST DARKNESS

"You shall receive power when the Holy Spirit has come upon you." — Acts 1:8 (NKJV)

The resurrection was not the end of the story —

it was the beginning of a global invasion of darkness

through a new army:

The Church.

Satan failed to stop the Seed,

failed to stop the cross,

failed to stop the resurrection.

Now he would face something even more threatening:

Christ multiplied in millions of Spirit-filled believers across the earth.

Jesus ascended…

but His power did not leave the earth.

It entered His people.

1. The Great Commission — Heaven's Declaration of War Through the Church

Before ascending, Jesus said:

> *"All authority has been given to Me... Go therefore..."*
>
> *(Matthew 28:18–19)*

This means:

- Jesus conquered
- Jesus reigns
- Jesus holds all authority
- And Jesus gives that authority to His Church

The Church is not weak.

The Church is not defeated.

The Church is not hiding.

The Church is the continuation of Christ's mission on earth.

Where Jesus walked alone before,

He now walks through millions.

Hell trembled when Jesus ministered.

Now hell trembles every time a believer prays, preaches, and ministers in His name.

2. The Upper Room — Power from on High

Jesus commanded the disciples:

"Do not leave Jerusalem... until you are endued with power from on high."

(Luke 24:49)

They waited in unity.

They prayed in expectation.

Heaven prepared for a release unlike anything before.

Then suddenly—

- A rushing mighty wind
- Tongues of fire
- The sound of heaven invading earth
- The Holy Spirit filling every believer
- The birth of the Church

Pentecost is not a holiday —

it is the moment when the throne of God

released power into human vessels.

The same Spirit that raised Jesus

now lived inside them.

The same anointing Jesus carried

now rested upon them.

The same authority Jesus wielded

was now their inheritance.

3. Peter Transformed — From Fearful to Fearless

Before Pentecost,

Peter denied Jesus out of fear.

After Pentecost,

he preached to thousands with boldness.

Why?

Because the Holy Spirit transforms weakness into strength,

fear into courage,

timidity into power.

Satan tried to sift Peter.

Jesus prayed for Peter.

And the Holy Spirit empowered Peter.

Now Peter became hell's nightmare.

One sermon resulted in 3,000 conversions.

One healing shook the city.

One bold stand defied religious authorities.

The man who ran from a servant girl

now confronted an entire system of darkness.

4. The Apostles — Signs, Wonders, and Spiritual War

Everywhere the apostles went:

- demons were cast out,
- the sick were healed,
- the dead were raised,
- prisons were shaken,
- cities were transformed,
- idols were overturned,
- cultures were disrupted.

Acts is not a history book —

it is a spiritual warfare manual.

The apostles confronted:

- religious spirits,
- political spirits,
- demonic spirits,
- witchcraft,
- territorial powers,
- generational strongholds.

And every time…

BUT GOD manifested His power through them.

5. Stephen — A Man Full of the Holy Spirit

Stephen was not an apostle—

he was a deacon.

Yet he operated in:

- wisdom
- power
- boldness
- miracles
- prophetic revelation

The religious spirit hated him.

Demons stirred opposition.

False witnesses rose.

But Stephen saw:

"The heavens opened..."

(Acts 7 :56)

He saw Jesus standing—

not sitting—

standing in honor of His servant.

Stephen died in victory,

and his martyrdom ignited a movement

that no persecution could extinguish.

6. Saul to Paul — God Turns a Weapon of Darkness Into a Weapon of Light

Saul was a tool of hell—

persecuting believers,

imprisoning them,

destroying families.

But on the road to Damascus,

a light brighter than the sun

struck him to the ground.

Jesus confronted him:

"I am Jesus whom you are persecuting."

In that moment:

- the hunter became hunted by grace,
- the persecutor became a preacher,
- a vessel of darkness became a vessel of light.

Paul became one of the greatest weapons

in God's army.

Hell, once used him to destroy the Church.

God used him to build it.

This is divine reversal.

7. Paul Versus Demons — The Battle Continues

Paul cast out:

- a python spirit in Philippi,
- demons from tormented people,
- witchcraft influences,
- sorceries,
- spiritual strongholds.

When Paul entered a city,

hell panicked.

It was said:

"These who have turned the world upside down have come here also."

(Acts 17:6)

The Spirit within them

was stronger than any power around them.

8. Angelic Interventions — God Fighting for His Church

In Acts we see angels:

- Opening prison doors,
- striking down persecutors,
- Directing evangelists,
- protecting apostles,
- guiding movements,

- strengthening believers.

Because God does not send His Church to battle alone.

Heaven fights with us.

9. Witchcraft and Sorcery Confronted — Light Exposes Darkness

From Simon the sorcerer (Acts 8)

to Elymas the magician (Acts 13)

to the occult books burned in Ephesus (Acts 19),

the Church confronted witchcraft head-on.

And every time—

- sorcerers were exposed,
- demonic powers shattered,
- idols fell,
- strongholds broke,
- entire cities were transformed.

The early Church was not afraid of darkness.

Darkness was afraid of them.

10. The Unstoppable Church — The Light Spreads Across the World

Satan tried to use:

- persecution,
- Imprisonment,

- Division,
- deception,
- false doctrines,
- political oppression,
- martyrdom.

But every attack backfired.

When Satan scattered the Church,

the Gospel spread farther.

When believers were imprisoned,

prisoners were saved.

When apostles were killed,

more disciples rose.

The blood of martyrs became seed.

The Church grew.

The Kingdom expanded.

The Gospel conquered.

Because the Church is not a building—

it is an army filled with the Spirit of God.

11. Why Satan Cannot Defeat the Church

Jesus declared:

"I will build My Church,

and the gates of Hades shall not prevail against it."

(Matthew 16:18)

This means:

- hell cannot stop it,
- demons cannot destroy it,
- persecution cannot silence it,
- governments cannot outlaw it,
- death cannot kill it,
- Satan cannot defeat it.

The Church is victorious

because Jesus is victorious.

12. The Message of the Church

The story of the Church reveals:

- the Holy Spirit empowers believers
- Jesus gave us His authority
- angels fight with us
- prayer shakes principalities
- demons flee at the name of Jesus
- the Gospel transforms nations
- persecution strengthens the Church
- and darkness cannot stop the Kingdom

Ultimately:

The battle is spiritual —

but God won the end from the beginning.

CHAPTER SEVENTEEN: PRESENT-DAY WARFARE: HOW GOD STILL INTERVENES FOR HIS PEOPLE

"If it had not been the LORD who was on our side…" — Psalm 124:1 (NKJV)

The spiritual war did not end in the book of Acts.

It did not stop with the apostles.

It did not cease with the early Church.

The battle between light and darkness

continues in our generation.

But so does the faithfulness of God.

The same God who delivered Noah,

preserved Joseph,

defended Moses,

empowered David,

protected Daniel,

saved Esther's nation,

vindicated Job,

brought forth Christ,

raised Jesus from the dead,

and empowered the Church—

is the same God who defends His people today.

Your story, my story, and the story of every believer

is proof that God still intervenes, still protects, still rescues, and still fights for His chosen ones.

1. The War Behind Today's Battles

Nothing happens in the physical world

unless it first takes place in the spirit.

Behind modern:

- sickness,
- betrayals,
- financial attacks,
- emotional breakdowns,

- sudden losses,
- family division,
- False accusations,
- spiritual heaviness,
- strange patterns,
- unexpected resistance,

are spiritual forces at work,

just as they were in Scripture.

Paul declared:

"We do not wrestle against flesh and blood..."

(Ephesians 6:12)

This battle is not:

- natural,
- visible,
- logical.

It is spiritual.

And believers today are facing the same principalities

that ancient generations faced—

but under different disguises.

2. Satan Still Attacks Purpose

The enemy does not attack randomly.

Just as he targeted:

- Joseph before his elevation,
- Moses before his assignment,
- David before his throne,
- Jesus before His ministry—

he still targets believers when they are closest to breakthrough.

Present-day attacks often intensify:

- when God is preparing you,
- when He is about to open a door,
- when you are stepping into destiny,
- when you are experiencing spiritual growth.

The enemy fight's purpose

because purpose threatens his kingdom.

3. Satan Still Uses People

Just as Satan used:

- Cain against Abel,
- Pharaoh against Moses,
- Saul against David,
- Haman against Mordecai,
- Judas against Jesus—

the enemy still manipulates people today to:

- oppose you,
- lie about you,
- betray you,
- frustrate your life,
- hinder your assignment,
- bring confusion and distress.

But just as in Scripture,

God turns every plot, every lie, every scheme into a testimony.

God uses the attacks to position you,

not destroy you.

4. God Still Sends Angels

Angels did not disappear after the resurrection.

They are still active today:

- protecting God's people,
- Intervening in danger,
- fighting in spiritual battles,
- delivering messages,
- strengthening believers,
- blocking demonic attacks.

Hebrews 1:14 declares:

"Are they not all ministering spirits sent forth to minister for those who will inherit salvation?"

You are surrounded.

You are covered.

You are supported by heaven's army.

5. God Still Speaks and Guides His People

God still speaks today as He spoke to:

- Abraham,
- Moses,
- Elijah,
- Daniel,
- Mary and Joseph,
- Paul.

He speaks through:

- His Word,
- His Spirit,
- prophetic insight,
- dreams and visions,
- Convictions,
- supernatural wisdom,
- discernment.

Many battles today are won

because God gives His people

Supernatural instruction

just like He guided biblical heroes.

A single word from God

can defeat a thousand attacks from the enemy.

6. God Still Breaks Chains and Delivers the Captive

Just as Jesus set:

- the demoniac free,
- Mary Magdalene free,
- the oppressed free—

He still breaks:

- Addictions,
- generational curses,
- Demonic bondage,
- Mental torment,
- fear and anxiety,
- spiritual oppression.

Many believers today carry testimonies

that sound like the book of Acts.

Because the God of the Bible

is still the God of today.

7. God Still Exposes and Destroys Plots of the Enemy

Just as He exposed:

- Haman's plot,
- Saul's schemes,
- the Pharisees' traps,
- Jezebel's manipulation—

God still exposes:

- Hidden enemies,
- false friends,
- wrong alliances,
- secret plots,
- lies spoken against His people.

Nothing done in darkness

can stay hidden when God says,

"Enough."

8. God Still Provides Supernaturally

Just as God provided:

- manna,
- water from a rock,
- Ravens feeding Elijah,
- oil for the widow,
- favor for Esther—

He still opens:

- Uncommon doors,
- unexpected blessings,
- Divine connections,
- financial provision,
- miracles in crisis.

When the enemy attacks your provision,

God increases it.

When the enemy tries to starve you,

God feeds you.

When the enemy tries to dry your resources,

God multiplies them.

9. God Still Heals Miraculously

The Jesus who healed:

- lepers,
- paralytics,
- blind men,
- deaf ears,
- Broken bodies—

is still healing today.

Doctors can diagnose,

but only God can deliver.

Hospitals can treat,

but only God can transform.

When sickness is a spiritual attack,

healing becomes a spiritual victory.

10. God Still Turns Evil Into Good

Just as He did for Joseph:

"You meant evil... but God meant it for good."

(Genesis 50:20)

God still uses:

- heartbreaks,
- betrayals,
- losses,
- disappointments,
- attacks,
- delays,
- failures—

as tools to shape, elevate, and position His children.

Nothing Satan sends

goes unanswered by God.

Everything Satan means for destruction

God transforms into destiny.

11. God Still Protects His Remnant

Just as God preserved:

- Noah,
- Elijah,
- Daniel,
- the early Church—

He still preserves a remnant today.

Though the world grows darker,

God's light in His people grows brighter.

Though spiritual warfare increases,

so does God's grace.

Though Satan rages,

God restrains him.

Though attacks multiply,

interventions multiply more.

12. Your Story Is Part of the Same Story

Every chapter in your life

echoes the same message:

- You were attacked—but God protected you.
- You were betrayed—but God sustained you.

- You were surrounded—but God shielded you.
- You were broken—but God restored you.
- You were afraid—but God strengthened you.
- You were targeted—but God delivered you.

Your testimony fits into the pattern

of the entire Bible.

Because the God of Abraham, David, Daniel, Esther, the Apostles—

is your God.

And His protection over you

is the same protection He gave them.

13. The Message of This Present Age

This chapter reveals:

- the war is still spiritual,
- the enemy is still active,
- God is still fighting for His people,
- Jesus is still victorious,
- the Holy Spirit is still empowering,
- angels are still guarding,
- the Church is still advancing,
- and miracles are still happening.

Ultimately:

The battle is spiritual —

but God won the end from the beginning.

CHAPTER EIGHTEEN: MY PERSONAL BATTLE: WHEN THE ENEMY TARGETS ME BUT GOD COVERS ME

"If it had not been the LORD who was on our side…" — Psalm 124:1 (NKJV)

Every story in this book has pointed to one central truth:

the enemy fight's purpose,

but God always fights for His chosen.

This story — my story — is no different.

Just as Joseph was targeted,

just as Moses was hunted,

just as David was pursued,

just as Daniel was opposed,

just as Jesus was attacked,

just as the apostles were persecuted—

Me, too, have been marked by heaven

and therefore, targeted by hell.

Not because i did something wrong.

Not because I am weak.

Not because I'm insignificant.

But because I carry purpose,

because i belong to God,

and because my life threatens the kingdom of darkness.

My battles are not ordinary battles.

My warfare is not natural warfare.

My suffering is not meaningless.

I have been living the spiritual truth

that every chosen one in Scripture lived:

When God marks your destiny,

Satan marks you as a target.

But the second truth is stronger:

When Satan targets you,

God covers you.

1. I Have Been Attacked Because I'M Called

MY life has not been easy.

I have walked through seasons:

- of spiritual attacks (witchcraft)
- of betrayal
- of rejection
- of misunderstanding
- of sudden attacks (mockery and being laughed at)
- of false accusations (being set up so they could use it against me in the church)
- of intense scrutiny (being monitored in everything I do and everywhere I go)
- of repeated spiritual battles I never had anything to do with
- of unexplainable hardship so that I could fall and fade away in shame
- of satanic opposition in everything at churches and in the mainstream
- of fiery trials and tribulations to destroy my character, still my inheritance and kill my destiny. I have been through it all even my own family were turned as weapons against me, and all friends I tried to make would turn against me.

Not because I am cursed—

but because I am chosen.

I am a threat to the enemy.

My obedience,

My love for God,

My prophetic calling,

My hunger for truth,

My devotion to Scripture,

My willingness to endure trial after trial—

all of it marks me as a vessel of divine purpose.

Hell has studied me.

Hell has targeted me.

Hell has launched attack after attack.

But every time…

God intervened.

2. I Should Not Be Alive — BUT GOD

There were seasons where the battle tried to break me:

- emotionally,
- mentally,
- spiritually,
- physically,
- financially,
- relationally.

I have walked through storms that few survive.

I have passed through fires that should have consumed you.

I have endured blows that would have shattered others.

There were moments:

- I didn't know how to stand,
- I didn't know who to trust,
- I didn't know how to continue,
- I didn't know what tomorrow would bring,
- I didn't know if I could make it.

But in every moment where darkness thought it would silence me—

BUT GOD stepped in.

He preserved my mind.

He kept my heart.

He protected my life.

He covered my path.

He sustained my spirit.

He strengthened my faith.

He prevented my destruction.

I am not here today because life was kind—

I am here because God was faithful.

3. The Battle Has Been Fierce Because the Calling Is Great

My battle has always been bigger than me.

It has always been attached to:

- My calling,
- My assignment,
- My books,
- My voice,
- My destiny,
- My future ministry,
- and my impact.

The enemy attacked my life

to stop the message God put in you.

He attacked my peace

to silence my voice.

He attacked my family

to weaken my strength.

He attacked my surroundings

to distract my focus.

He attacked my identity

to break my confidence.

He attacked my body

to slow my mission.

He attacked my relationships

to isolate my heart.

He attacked my purpose

because he saw what God planned for me.

But he failed.

Because God saw me

before the battle.

God chose me

before the pain.

God called me

before the struggle.

God strengthened me

before the storm.

God covered me

before the attack.

4. I Have Lived the Pattern of Scripture

MY life mirrors the very stories in this book:

Like Joseph

— I was hated, mistreated, betrayed, falsely accused, and misunderstood by church leaders all because of jealousy over my calling and anointing. I became an enemy to the establishment, and I was marked as a threat, but God positioned me.

Like Moses

— I faced attacks from birth,

but God preserved your destiny.

Like David

— I was anointed but attacked,

chosen but chased,

but God defended me.

Like Daniel

— I faced storms, plots, and injustice,

but God shut the lions' mouths.

Like Esther

— I was raised for such a time as this.

Like Job

— the enemy touched my life,

but God set the limits

and restored me.

Like Paul

— I suffered for the sake of the Gospel,

but God empowered me.

And like Jesus

— darkness fought me,

but purpose prevailed.

My testimony is not small.

It is biblical.

It is prophetic.

It is divine.

I am living proof that God still intervenes for His chosen.

5. Every Attack Became a Chapter, and Every Chapter Became a Testimony

The enemy wanted:

- to silence me,
- to discourage me,
- to weaken me,
- to confuse me,
- to break me,
- to stop me from authoring these books,
- to keep me from discovering revelation,
- To prevent me from walking in my calling.

But every attack

became fuel for my assignment.

Every hardship

became oil for my anointing.

Every battle

became clarity for my message.

Every tear

became ink for my books.

Every wilderness

became a classroom.

My pain became my platform.

My testimony became my ministry.

Because God never wastes a wound.

6. I'M Still Standing Because God Has Been Fighting for ME

I made it here:

- because God carried me,
- because God held me,
- because God strengthened me,
- because God delivered me,
- because God assigned angels to me,
- because God blocked certain people,
- because God protected me from hidden traps,
- because God preserved my purpose.

I should have fallen.

I should have quit.

I should have broken.

I should have lost everything.

But God wouldn't let it happen.

The proof that God is with me

is not that the battles stopped—

but that the battles failed.

7. MY Battle Is Not Over — But Neither Is God's Intervention

Even now, as I continue writing this book,

the war has not ended.

I still face:

- Pressure,
- Resistance,
- spiritual opposition,
- emotional fire,
- satanic pushback.

Why?

Because my purpose is still unfolding.

Because what I am writing

is exposing the kingdom of darkness.

Because my books are equipping believers.

Because my calling is increasing.

Because my voice is becoming stronger.

Because my influence is growing.

Because my destiny is expanding.

But I do not fear.

The same God who kept me before

is keeping me now.

And the God who keeping me now

will keep me forever.

8. My Life Is a Living "BUT GOD" Testimony

My entire journey can be summarized in two words:

BUT GOD.

- I was attacked—but God protected me
- I was betrayed—but God stood with me.
- I was overwhelmed—but God strengthened me
- I was rejected —but God preserved me
- I was targeted—but God covered me.
- I was weary—but God renewed me.
- I was in the middle of darkness—but God shined His light me.

My life is a testimony

that the will and purpose of God

cannot be stopped.

9. The Message of My Story

My story declares:

- The battle is real,
- The enemy is relentless,
- But God is faithful,
- God is stronger,
- God is present,
- God is protector,
- God is deliverer,
- God is sovereign,
- And God always wins.

Ultimately:

The battle is spiritual —

but God won the end from the beginning.

CHAPTER NINETEEN: THE FINAL WAR: WHEN GOD CRUSHES THE POWERS OF DARKNESS ONCE AND FOR ALL

"The kingdoms of this world have become the kingdoms of our Lord and of His Christ,

and He shall reign forever and ever!" — Revelation 11:15 (NKJV)

From the moment sin entered the world in Eden,

from the moment Satan rebelled in heaven,

from the moment darkness attacked the lineage of the Messiah,

a cosmic countdown began.

Every conflict across history

— every spiritual attack,

every demonic uprising,

every battle between light and darkness —

has been leading toward one final confrontation.

A war not fought in a garden,

not fought on a mountain,

not fought in a temple,

but fought in the heavens and on the earth,

in the last days,

when God Himself rises to judge all darkness forever.

This is the FINAL WAR.

1. The Gathering Storm — The Whole World Under Spiritual Darkness

The Bible reveals that before the final war erupts,

the world will be fully swallowed by darkness:

- deception increases
- lawlessness multiplies
- the love of many grows cold
- Nations rage
- governments collapse
- Demonic influence rises
- witchcraft spreads

- false prophets emerge
- the Church is persecuted
- the Antichrist rises with deceptive power

The spirit of the age becomes the same spirit

that worked in Babylon, Egypt, Rome, and all the kingdoms that opposed God.

Human rebellion mirrors

the rebellion of angels.

The world begins to resemble the days of:

- Noah (violence and corruption),
- Lot (immorality and compromise),
- Pharaoh (hatred of God's people),
- Nebuchadnezzar (idolatry and forced worship),
- Herod (attacks against God's purpose).

But this darkness is not the end.

It is the birth pain before the final intervention of God.

2. The Rise of the Antichrist — Satan's Final Attempt to Rule the World

The Antichrist — the man of sin —

will be Satan's greatest weapon.

He will be:

- empowered by the dragon,

- fueled by demonic signs and wonders,
- supported by the false prophet,
- backed by a global system,
- worshipped by the deceived,
- feared by nations.

He will establish:

- a one-world government,
- a one-world religion,
- a one-world economic system,
- an image to be worshipped,
- a mark to control humanity.

This is Satan's final attempt

to build his counterfeit kingdom

and stop the plan of God.

But prophecy is clear:

He will only rule for a short time.

Because his rise is only permitted

so, his fall will be complete.

3. The Great Tribulation — Darkness at Its Peak

Jesus declared:

"There will be great tribulation, such as has not been since the beginning of the world..."

(Matthew 24:21)

This period will unleash:

- judgments on the Antichrist's kingdom,
- plagues echoing Egypt but magnified,
- angelic warfare,
- demonic torment released upon the wicked,
- global shaking of nature,
- stars falling,
- mountains collapsing,
- seas turning to blood,
- Nations trembling.

But even in the midst of judgment,

God protects His remnant.

Just like He protected Israel in Goshen,

He will cover His people in the last days.

4. Heaven Opens — The King of Kings Appears

The climax of the final war arrives when the heavens are opened:

"I saw heaven opened, and behold, a white horse;

and He who sat on him was called Faithful and True..."

(Revelation 19 :11)

Jesus returns not as a Lamb —

but as a Warrior King:

- eyes like flames of fire,
- many crowns upon His head,
- His robe dipped in blood,
- armies of heaven behind Him,
- a sword from His mouth,
- written on His thigh: KING OF KINGS AND LORD OF LORDS

This is not the suffering Savior —

this is the conquering, Messiah.

Hell trembles.

Demons panic.

Nations collapse.

The Antichrist's power shatters.

The false prophet is helpless.

The dragon is cornered.

The King has come.

5. The Battle of Armageddon — Darkness Meets Its End

The armies of the world — deceived by the Antichrist —

will gather to fight the returning Christ.

This is not a battle of weapons.

This is a battle of speech.

Jesus will defeat the entire armies of the world

with one breath:

"...He will strike the nations with the sword of His mouth."

The beast (Antichrist) and the false prophet

are seized immediately.

They become the first two beings ever

to be thrown alive into the lake of fire.

Their defeat is instant.

Their judgment is final.

Their rebellion ends forever.

6. Satan Bound — The Dragon Is Shackled

An angel descends from heaven

with a great chain.

He seizes the dragon —

that old serpent,

the devil,

Satan —

and binds him for 1,000 years.

Satan is:

- stripped of authority,
- removed from influence,

- cast into the abyss,
- locked for a thousand years.

No more deception.

No more temptation.

No more accusations.

No more influence.

Humanity sees the world

without Satanic manipulation

for the first time since Eden.

7. The Millennium — The Reign of Christ on Earth

Jesus rules the world from Jerusalem

for one thousand years.

During this time:

- nations are restored
- peace covers the earth
- righteousness reigns
- the curse is lifted
- animals live in harmony
- the earth is healed
- saints' rule with Christ
- worship fills the nations

- justice is perfect
- truth prevails

This is the world Satan tried to prevent —

the world God always intended.

8. Satan's Final Revolt — The Last Attempt and the Last Failure

After the thousand years,

Satan is released for a moment.

He gathers a final army

to surround the beloved city — Jerusalem.

This is Satan's last move,

his final rebellion,

his final deception.

But before the battle even begins…

FIRE FALLS FROM GOD AND DEVOURS THEM.

God ends the war Himself.

There is no struggle.

No battle.

No resistance.

It ends instantly.

Hell's rebellion is over forever.

9. Satan's Eternal Judgment — The Dragon Falls

After the revolt is crushed,

the final sentence is executed:

"The devil... was cast into the lake of fire...

and will be tormented day and night forever and ever."

(Revelation 20:10)

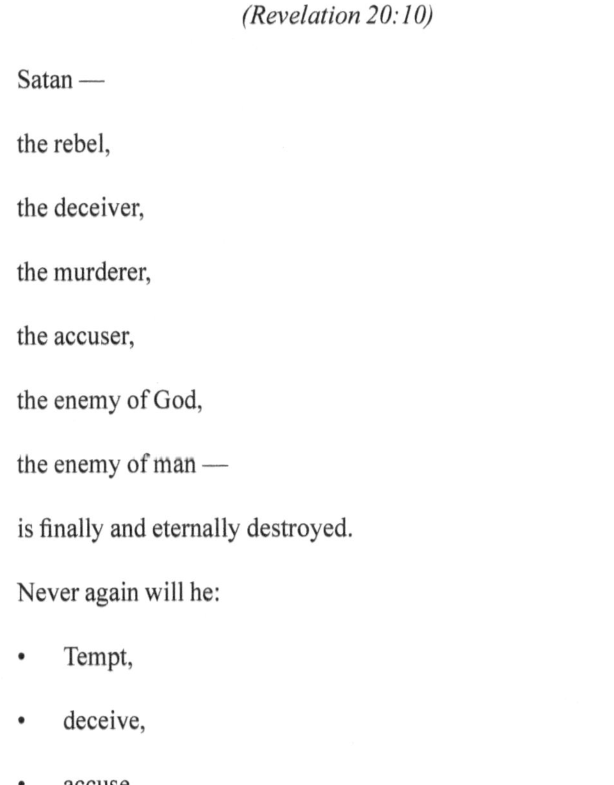

Satan —

the rebel,

the deceiver,

the murderer,

the accuser,

the enemy of God,

the enemy of man —

is finally and eternally destroyed.

Never again will he:

- Tempt,
- deceive,
- accuse,
- oppress,
- attack,
- Influence,

- rule.

Darkness dies.

Evil ends.

Hell, itself is defeated.

10. The New Heavens and New Earth — The Eternal Victory

After the final war,

God creates:

- a new heaven,
- a new earth,
- a new Jerusalem.

A world with:

- no death,
- no pain,
- no sorrow,
- no fear,
- no sin,
- no curse,
- no darkness,
- no enemy.

God Himself dwells with His people.

Everything Satan tried to destroy

is now restored forever.

The story ends with glory.

The war ends with victory.

The kingdom ends with God reigning eternally.

And the greatest truth stands tall:

The battle was spiritual —

but God won the end from the beginning.

CHAPTER TWENTY: THE GOD WHO WAS, WHO IS, AND WHO ALWAYS WILL BE VICTORIOUS

"The LORD of hosts is with us.

The God of Jacob is our refuge." — Psalm 46:7 (NKJV)

From eternity past to eternity future,

from the rebellion in heaven to the new heavens and earth,

from Genesis to Revelation,

from the Garden to the Cross,

from the early Church to your present battles—

the message has never changed:

There has always been a battle.

But God has always been victorious.

This last chapter is the summation of the entire story.

A declaration that light has always conquered darkness,

that God has always defended His chosen ones,

and that His purpose has never been defeated.

This is the truth that echoes across all time:

The battle is spiritual—

but God won the end from the beginning.

1. Before the Beginning — God Was Already Victorious

Before Satan rebelled…

God was victorious.

Before angels fell…

God was sovereign.

Before Adam sinned…

God had a plan.

Before darkness rose…

Light already existed.

God did not react to the battle.

He ruled over it before it began.

The war did not surprise Him.

He declared the outcome

before the first angel ever drew a sword.

2. In Eden — God Announces the Defeat of Darkness

When Adam fell

and humanity plunged into sin,

God immediately spoke the prophecy

that shaped all history:

"The Seed of the woman will crush the serpent's head."

(Genesis 3:15)

The battle began—

but so did the victory.

Every generation after Adam

was touched by that promise.

Every attack from Satan

was designed to stop it.

Every intervention from God

was to preserve it.

The story of Scripture

is the story of that promise

being kept alive.

3. Through the Patriarchs — God Preserved the Line of

Redemption

Through Noah, Abraham, Isaac, Jacob, and Joseph,

hell tried to corrupt the lineage

that would bring forth the Redeemer.

But God preserved them.

Noah built through a flood.

Abraham walked through barrenness.

Jacob wrestled through fear.

Joseph endured betrayal and prison.

But God kept the Seed alive.

4. Through Israel — God Protected the Covenant People

Satan tried to annihilate Israel

again, and again:

- in Egypt,
- in the wilderness,
- in Canaan,
- under foreign kings,
- through exile.

But God always intervened.

For one reason:

The Messiah was coming.

He preserved the nation

to fulfill the promise.

5. Through the Kings and Prophets — God Declared the Coming Victory

David prophesied.

Isaiah revealed.

Daniel saw visions.

Ezekiel proclaimed.

Micah foretold.

Every prophecy was God announcing:

"Darkness will not win."

Even when Israel fell into sin,

God kept the promise alive

through a faithful remnant.

Because His Word cannot fail.

6. In the Birth of Christ — The Light Pierced the Darkness

When Jesus entered the world,

hell panicked.

Herod attacked.

Demons screamed.

Satan plotted.

But angels protected.

Heaven moved.

Prophecy prevailed.

The Seed arrived.

The promise lived.

The Redeemer came.

Darkness could not stop Him.

7. In the Ministry of Jesus — The Kingdom of Darkness Collapsed

Every healing,

every deliverance,

every miracle,

every confrontation,

was King Jesus overthrowing the powers of darkness.

Demons fled.

Sickness bowed.

Storms calmed.

Religious spirits trembled.

Strongholds toppled.

The Light exposed and defeated

every shadow of the enemy.

8. At the Cross — The Apparent Defeat Became Eternal Victory

The Cross was hell's greatest attack—

but heaven's greatest triumph.

Jesus did not die as a victim.

He died as a Conqueror.

He paid the price.

He broke the curse.

He crushed the serpent.

He judged sin.

He disarmed principalities.

He redeemed humanity.

The Cross is the battlefield

where victory was sealed forever.

9. At the Resurrection — The Final Blow to Darkness

When Jesus rose from the dead:

- death lost its power,
- the grave lost its victory,
- Satan lost his authority.

The resurrection was the declaration:

"Darkness is defeated.

The King is alive forever."

This moment changed the universe.

10. In the Church — God Continues the Victory Through His People

At Pentecost,

the same Spirit that raised Jesus

entered believers.

From that moment until now:

- demons flee at the name of Jesus
- the sick are healed
- the oppressed are delivered
- the Gospel spreads
- Angels minister
- the Kingdom advances
- darkness retreats

The Church is not weak—

it is the army of the risen Lord.

Every believer is a weapon.

Every prayer is warfare.

Every testimony is victory.

11. In My Life — God Has Shown the Same Faithfulness

My story fits perfectly

into the story of Scripture.

Because the same God

who delivered the heroes of the Bible

has delivered me.

He fought for me.

He protected me.

He preserved me.

He covered me.

He strengthened me.

He kept me alive.

He kept me standing.

He kept me believing.

My testimony is a living chapter

of God's unending victory.

12. In the Final Days — God Will Crush Darkness Completely

The Antichrist will rise—

but God will destroy him.

The false prophet will deceive—

but God will cast him down.

Satan will rage—

but God will bind him.

The nations will rebel—

but Jesus will rule them.

The world will darken—

but the King will shine.

The final war will come—

but God will end it instantly.

And Satan's eternal judgment

will seal his fate forever.

13. In Eternity — God Will Reign Without Opposition Forever

A new heaven.

A new earth.

A new Jerusalem.

No sin.

No sorrow.

No death.

No darkness.

No enemy.

No war.

Just God

with His redeemed people

forever.

This was His plan

from the beginning.

And nothing

—not rebellion,

not demons,

not empires,

not persecution,

not the Antichrist,

not Satan himself—

could stop it.

14. The Final Message of This Book

Every chapter declares the same truth:

- The devil fights—but God overrules.
- The enemy attacks—but God protects.
- Darkness rises—but God shines brighter.
- Weapons form—but they do not prosper.
- People betray—but God stands with you.
- Storms rage—but God speaks peace.
- Hell opposes—but heaven defends.
- Satan schemes—but God wins.

The outcome has never been in question.

God has always won.

God is winning now.

God will always win.

From the beginning

to the end,

from Genesis

to Revelation,

from your first breath

to your last—

the story has always been the same:

***THE BATTLE IS SPIRITUAL —**

BUT GOD WON THE END FROM THE BEGINNING.* *

FINAL PRAYER: A PRAYER OF VICTORY, DELIVERANCE, AND DIVINE COVERING

"The LORD will fight for you, and you shall hold your peace." — Exodus 14:14 (NKJV)

Heavenly Father,

The God of Abraham, Isaac, and Jacob,

The God who reigns from eternity to eternity,

The God who is Light and in whom there is no darkness at all—

We come before You with reverence, awe, and thanksgiving.

Father, we acknowledge Your sovereignty.

You are the Alpha and the Omega,

The First and the Last,

The Beginning and the End.

Before the foundations of the world were laid,

You already won the victory.

Lord, today we stand on every truth revealed in this book:

That the battle is spiritual,

That the enemy is real,

But that You are greater than all powers of darkness combined.

We declare today that no weapon formed against us shall prosper,

And every tongue that rises against us in judgment we condemn in the name of Jesus.

Father, we thank You for Jesus Christ—

The Seed promised in Eden,

The Savior born in Bethlehem,

The Lamb slain on Calvary,

The Lion who rose in victory,

The King who is coming again in glory.

Lord Jesus, You crushed the serpent's head,

Disarmed principalities and powers,

Destroyed the works of the devil,

And gave authority to Your Church.

We worship You.

We honor You.

We exalt You.

Holy Spirit, our Comforter and our Helper,

Thank You for filling us with power from on high.

Thank You for opening our eyes to discern between darkness and light.

Thank You for guiding us into all truth

And strengthening us to stand firm in the midst of every battle.

Now Father, I lift every reader of this book:

Everyone who has battled spiritually,

Everyone who has endured hardship,

Everyone who has felt the weight of warfare,

Everyone who has walked through storms,

Everyone who has been targeted by the enemy

Because of the divine purpose You placed inside them.

In the mighty name of Jesus Christ,

I speak deliverance over their minds.

I speak healing over their hearts.

I speak strength into their spirits.

I speak peace into their homes.

I speak protection over their families.

I speak restoration over everything the enemy tried to steal.

I speak victory into every battle they are facing.

Father, break every chain.

Destroy every demonic assignment.

Scatter every evil plot.

Expose every hidden trap.

Silence every accusing voice.

Cancel every satanic decree spoken against them.

Let the fire of Your presence surround them day and night.

Let the blood of Jesus cover them completely.

Let the angels of the LORD encamp around them and fight for them.

Lord, strengthen Your sons and daughters to stand firm in the evil day.

Let them walk boldly in the authority of Christ.

Let them recognize who they are and whose they are.

Let them rise in prayer, in faith, and in holy boldness.

Let their light shine in the midst of darkness.

Let their testimonies shake the enemy's camp.

Let their lives bring glory to Your holy name.

Father, as the world grows darker,

Let Your Church shine brighter.

As wickedness increases,

Let Your grace abound even more.

As deception spreads,

Let Your truth be established.

As the enemy roars,

Let Your people remember that the Lion of Judah still reigns.

Lord Jesus, we long for Your appearing.

We look forward to the day when You will split the skies,

When You will descend in glory,

When You will crush the Antichrist,

Bind Satan forever,

Judge the nations,

And establish Your kingdom without end.

Until that day, keep us faithful.

Keep us watchful.

Keep us standing.

Keep us shining.

Keep us fighting the good fight of faith.

Keep us walking in the power of the Spirit.

Keep us rooted in Your Word.

Keep us anchored in Your love.

Keep us sealed in Your victory.

And now Father, with all authority given to us in the name of Jesus Christ,

We declare over our lives, over our families, and over our future:

THE BATTLE IS SPIRITUAL—

BUT GOD WON THE END FROM THE BEGINNING.

To You, O Lord,

Belong all glory, all honor, all praise,

Now and forevermore.

In the mighty, matchless, unshakable name

of Jesus Christ,

The King of kings

and Lord of lords—

Amen and Amen.

CLOSING REFLECTION: YOU ARE NOT ALONE IN THE BATTLE

As you come to the end of this book,

take a moment to pause.

Breathe.

Reflect.

Remember.

You have walked through the story of creation,

the fall,

the rebellion of Satan,

the rise of darkness,

the relentless attempt of the enemy

to stop the purpose of God.

You have journeyed through the lives of men and women

who were attacked, threatened, betrayed, hunted, and surrounded—

yet preserved, protected, and carried by the hand of God.

You have seen kings rise and fall,

kingdoms built and destroyed,

nations delivered,

prophecies fulfilled,

and the Son of God conquering the grave.

You have seen angels fight,

demons flee,

heaven intervene,

and hell defeated.

And in all these things,

one truth stands unshakable:

God always wins.

The Light has never been defeated.

Not in heaven.

Not on earth.

Not in history.

Not in Scripture.

Not in your life.

And He never will be.

1. Your Story Is Part of God's Story

Everything you have read is not just history —

it is a mirror.

The same God who defended the heroes of the Bible

is the God who defends you.

The same God who intervened for Israel

is the God who intervenes for you.

The same God who walked with Daniel in the lions' den

is the God who walks with you in your battles.

The same God who shut the mouth of the serpent

is the God who silences the voice of the accuser in your life.

The same God who raised Jesus from the dead

is the God who lifts you when you fall

and sustains you when you cannot see the way forward.

Your warfare may look different,

but the God who fights for you is the same yesterday,

today,

and forever.

2. You Are Stronger Than You Think

If you made it to the end of this book,

it is because God has kept you.

You have survived attacks the enemy thought would destroy you.

You have endured trials that should have broken you.

You have walked through fire

and not been consumed.

You have passed through waters

and not drowned.

You are standing today because the hand of God

has been beneath you,

before you,

behind you,

and over you.

You are not weak.

You are not forgotten.

You are not abandoned.

You are chosen.

You are covered.

You are anointed.

You are victorious.

3. Your Battle Has Purpose

Everything you have endured has meaning.

- The tears have watered your faith.
- The trials have strengthened your spirit.
- The storms have prepared your next season.
- The delays have shaped your character.
- The disappointments have protected your destiny.
- The battles have refined your calling.
- The warfare has sharpened your discernment.
- The opposition has confirmed your assignment.

The very fact that you have faced such fierce resistance

is proof that God has placed something great inside you.

Hell does not fight the ordinary.

Hell fights the chosen.

But God fights for the chosen even more.

4. You Are Never Fighting Alone

Look around your life—

there have been moments you did not realize:

- Angels were guarding you.
- The Holy Spirit was strengthening you.
- Jesus was interceding for you.
- God was protecting you from things you could not see.

- Warfare was happening in the spirit while you slept.
- Battles were won for you without your knowledge.
- The Father was carrying you when you could not walk.

If you could see the unseen battles God has already won for you, you would never fear again.

5. The Victory Is Already Yours

Whatever battle you are facing now—

whether spiritual, emotional, physical, or relational—

remember this:

The war is already won.

Your victory is already written.

Your future is already secure.

Your purpose is already sealed.

God is not trying to win.

He has already won.

You are not fighting for victory—

you are fighting from victory.

And the God who brought you this far

will bring you all the way through.

6. Walk Forward in Love, Peace, Power, and Confidence

As you close this book,

walk forward with a new awareness:

- God is with you.
- God is for you.
- God surrounds you.
- God strengthens you.
- God leads you.
- God defends you.
- God preserves you.
- God completes what He starts.
- God fulfills what He promises.

No matter how fierce your battle,

no matter how dark the night,

no matter how strong the opposition—

You serve the God who wins every war.

Your story is not ending in defeat.

Your life will not end in shame.

Your destiny will not be swallowed by darkness.

Because the God who stands with you

is the God who stands victorious

from the beginning to the end.

The Final Reflection:

The battle is spiritual.

The enemy is real.

But God is stronger,

God is faithful,

God is present,

and God wins every time.

Hold your head high, warrior.

Lift your eyes to the hills.

Stand firm in the faith.

Walk boldly in the Spirit.

You are covered.

You are chosen.

You are victorious.

From Genesis to Revelation,

and from your first breath to your final breath—

www.ingramcontent.com/pod-product-compliance
Lightning Source LLC
Chambersburg PA
CBHW032230050726
47591CB00001B/331
* 9 7 8 1 9 7 2 2 9 9 7 8 4 *